Nooks and Corners of Old New York

Nooks and Corners of Old New York

Charles Hemstreet

Illustrated by

E. C. Peixotto, with Additional Historic Maps, Photos, and Illustrations

With a New Afterword by Ken Bloom

EXCELSIOR EDITIONS

Cover Art credit line: 1609. The island of Manhattan at the time of its discovery showing its elevations, water-courses, marshes, and shore line. Lionel Pincus and Princess Firyal Map Division, The New York Public Library, NYPL Digital Collections.

Originally published by Charles Scribner's Sons, 1899.
Published by State University of New York Press, Albany

Printed in the United States of America

Excelsior Editions is an imprint of State University of New York Press
For information, contact State University of New York Press, Albany, NY
www.sunypress.edu

Library of Congress Cataloging-in-Publication Data
Names: Hemstreet, Charles, 1866- author. | Peixotto, Ernest C., 1869-1940, illustrator. | Bloom, Ken, 1949- writer of afterword.
Title: Nooks and corners of old New York / Charles Hemstreet ; illustrated by E.C. Peixotto, with additional historic maps, photos, and illustrations ; with a new afterword by Ken Bloom.
Description: Albany : State University of New York Press, [2023] | Series: New York classics | Original title: Nooks & corners of old New York. | Includes bibliographical references and index.
Identifiers: LCCN 2022062261 | ISBN 9781438495002 (hardcover) | ISBN 9781438494999 (paperback) | ISBN 9781438495019 (ebook)
Subjects: LCSH: New York (N.Y.)--Buildings, structures, etc.--History. | Historic buildings--New York (State)--New York--History. | New York (N.Y.)--History. | New York (N.Y.)--Description and travel.
Classification: LCC F128.37 .H49 2023 | DDC 974.7/1--dc23/eng/20230104
LC record available at https://lccn.loc.gov/2022062261

10 9 8 7 6 5 4 3 2 1

CONTENTS

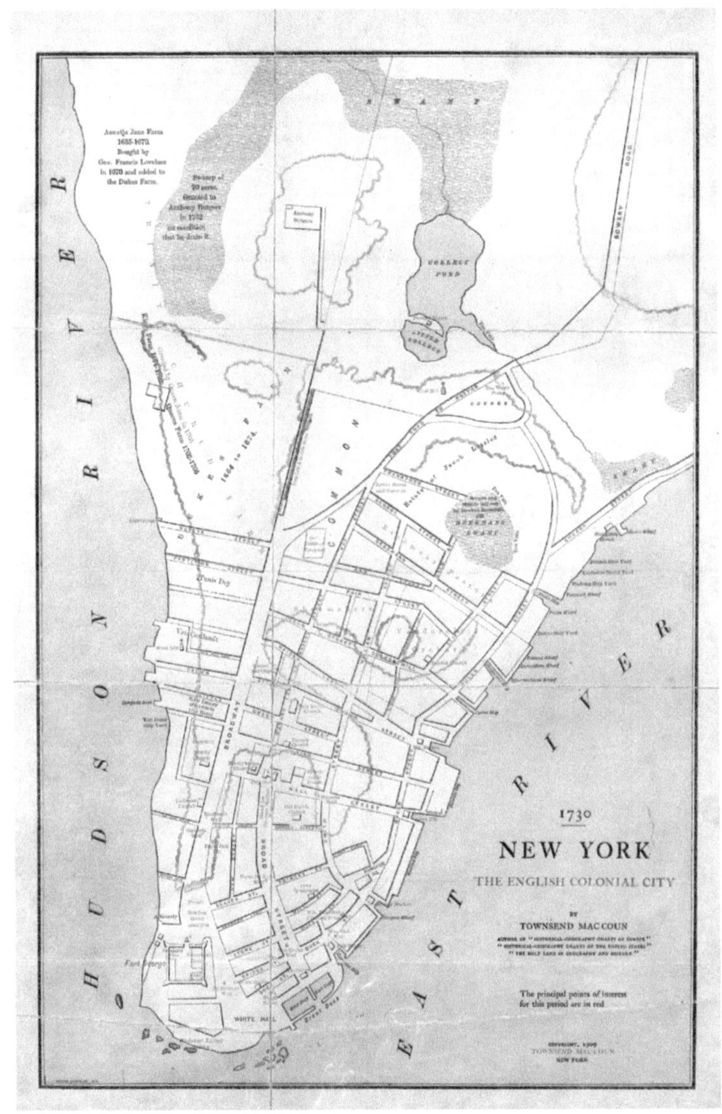

Map of Colonial Era New York, c. 1730. Lionel Pincus and Princess Firyal Map Division, NYPL Digital Collections.

INTRODUCTORY NOTE

The points of interest referred to in this book are to be found in the lower part of the Island of Manhattan.

Settlements having early been made in widely separated parts of the island, streets were laid out from each settlement as they were needed without regard to the city as a whole; with the result that as the city grew the streets lengthened and those of the various sections met.at every conceivable angle. This resulted in a tangle detrimental to the city's interests, and in 1807 a Commission was appointed to devise a City Plan that should protect the interests of the *whole* community.

A glance at a city map will show the confusion of streets at the lower end of the island and the regularity brought about under the City Plan above Houston Street on the east, and Fourteenth Street on the west side.

The plan adopted by the Commission absolutely disregarded the natural topography of the island, and resulted in a city of straight lines and right angles.

LIST OF ILLUSTRATIONS

Nooks and Corners of Old New York

I

Fort Amsterdam

On the centre building of the row which faces Bowling Green Park on the south there is a tablet bearing the words:

> THE SITE OF FORT AMSTERDAM, BUILT IN 1626.
> WITHIN THE FORTIFICATIONS WAS ERECTED
> THE FIRST
> SUBSTANTIAL CHURCH EDIFICE ON THE ISLAND
> OF MANHATTAN.
> IN 1787 THE FORT
> WAS DEMOLISHED
> AND THE GOVERNMENT HOUSE BUILT UPON THIS SITE

This was the starting-point of the Dutch West India Co. settlement which gradually became New York. In 1614 a stockade, called Fort Manhattan, was built as a temporary place of shelter for representatives of the United New Netherland Co., which had been formed to trade with the Indians. This company was replaced by the Dutch West India Co., with chartered rights to trade on the American coast, and the first step towards the forming of a permanent settlement was the building of Fort Amsterdam on the site of the stockade.

Fort Amsterdam. Nieuw Nederlandt. Henry R. Robinson, lithographer. The Miriam and Ira D. Wallach Division of Art, Prints and Photographs: Picture Collection, NYPL Digital Collections.

In 1664 New Amsterdam passed into British possession and became New York, while Fort Amsterdam became Fort James. Under Queen Anne it was Fort George, remaining so until demolished in 1787.

On the Fort's site was built the Government House, intended for Washington and the Presidents who should follow him. But none ever occupied it as the seat of government was removed to Philadelphia before the house was completed. After 1801 it became an office building, and was demolished in 1815 to make room for the present structures.

Bowling Green

The tiny patch of grass at the starting-point of Broadway, now called Bowling Green Park, was originally the centre of sports for colonists, and has been the scene of many stirring events. The iron railing which now surrounds it was set up in 1771, having been imported from England to enclose a lead equestrian statue of King George III. On the posts of the fence were representations of heads of members of the Royal family. In 1776, during the Revolution, the statue was dragged down and molded into bullets, and where the iron heads were knocked from the posts the fracture can still be seen.

The Battery

When the English took possession of the city, in 1664, the Fort being regarded as useless, it was decided to build a Battery to protect the newly acquired possession. Thus the idea of the Battery was conceived, although the work was not actually carried out until 1684.

Beyond the Fort there was a fringe of land with the water reaching to a point within a line drawn from Water and Whitehall Streets to Greenwich Street. Sixty years after the Battery was built fifty guns were added, it having been lightly armed up to that time. The Battery was demolished about the same time as the Fort. The land on which it stood became a small park, retaining the name of the Battery, and was gradually added to until it became the Battery Park of to-day.

Castle Garden

A small island, two hundred feet off the Battery, to which it was connected by a drawbridge, was fortified in 1811 and called Fort Clinton. The armament was twenty-eight 32 -pounders, none of which was ever fired at an enemy. In 1822 the island was ceded back to the city by the Federal Government—when the military headquarters were transferred to Governor's Island and became a place of amusement under the name of Castle Garden. It was the first real home of opera in America. General Lafayette was received there in 1824, and there Samuel F. B. Morse first demonstrated the possibility of controlling an electric current in 1835. Jenny Lind, under the management of P. T. Barnum, appeared there in 1850. In 1855 it became a depot for the reception of immigrants; in 1890 the offices were removed to Ellis Island, and in 1896, after many postponements, Castle Garden was opened as a public aquarium.

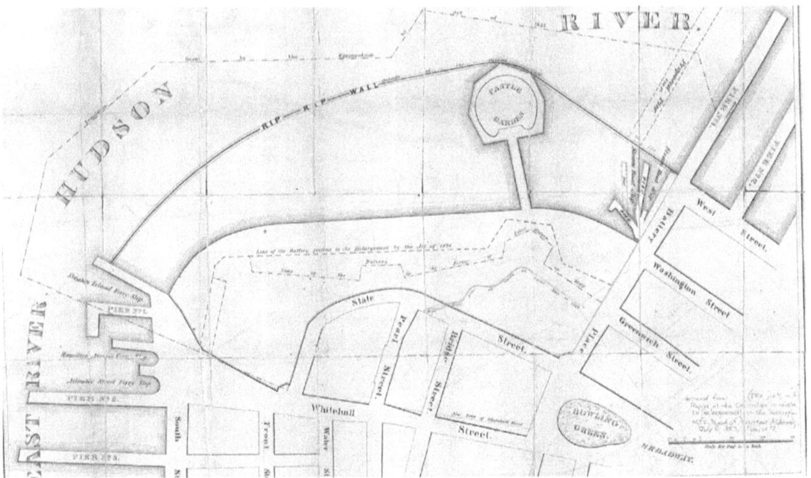

Map of the Bowery, 1853. Lionel Pincus and Princess Firyal Map Division, NYPL Digital Collections.

State Street

State Street, facing the Battery, during the latter part of the eighteenth and the early part of the nineteenth century, was the fashionable quarter of the city, and on it were the homes of the wealthy. Several of the old houses still survive. No. 7, now a home for immigrant Irish girls, was the most conspicuous on the street, and is in about its original state. At No. 9 lived John Morton, called the "rebel banker" by the British, because he loaned large sums to the Continental Congress. His son, General Jacob Morton, occupied the mansion after his marriage in 1791, and commanded the militia. Long after he became too infirm to actually command, from the balcony of his home he reviewed on the Battery parade grounds the Tompkins Blues and the Light Guards. The veterans of these commands, by legislative enactment in 1868, were incorporated as the "Old Guard."

Nº 7 *State Street*

The "Stadhuis"

On the building at 4 and 6 Pearl Street, corner State Street, is a tablet which reads:

1636 1897
ON THIS SITE STOOD THE "STADHUIS"
OF NEW AMSTERDAM—ERECTED 1636
THIS TABLET IS PLACED HERE IN LOVING MEMORY
OF THE FIRST DUTCH SETTLERS BY THE
HOLLAND DAMES OF THE NEW
NETHERLANDS AND THE KNIGHTS OF THE LEGION
OF THE CROWN
LAVINIA
KONIGIN

It was set up October 7, 1897, and marks the supposed site of the first City Hall. What is claimed by most authorities to be the real site is at Pearl Street, opposite Coenties Slip.

Whitehall Street was one of the earliest thoroughfares of the city, and was originally the open space left on the land side of the Fort.

Beaver Street was first called the Beaver's Path. It was a ditch, on either side of which was a path. When houses were built along these paths they were improved by a rough pavement. At the end of the Beaver's Path, close to where Broad Street is now, was a swamp, which, before the pavements were made, had been reclaimed and was known as the Sheep Pasture.

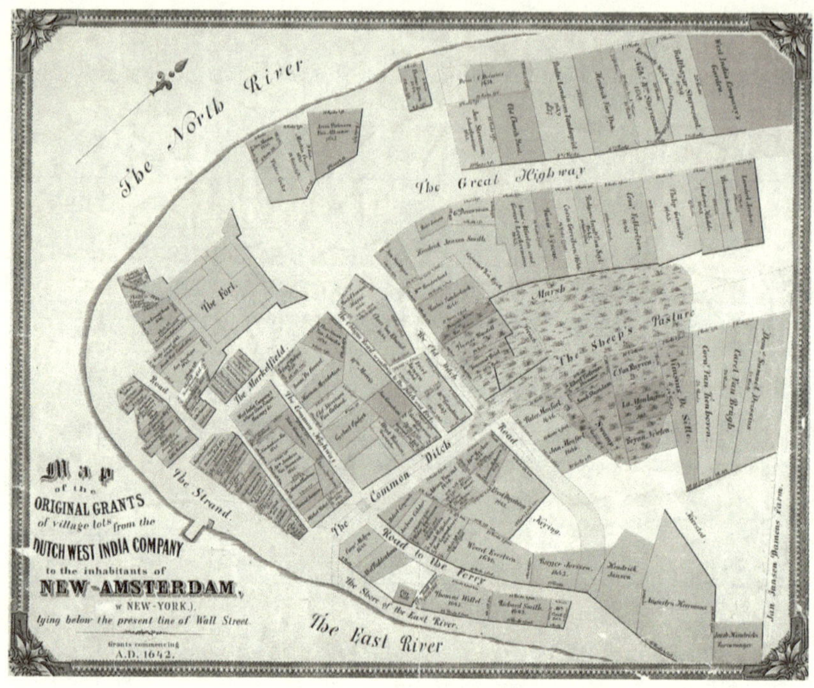

Map of the original land grants from the Dutch West India Company to the inhabitants of New-Amsterdam, showing the sheep pasture and other early locations. Henry Dunreath Tyler, cartographer. Lionel Pincus and Princess Firyal Map Division, NYPL Digital Collections.

Petticoat Lane

Marketfield Street, whose length is less than a block, opens into Broad Street at no. 72, a few feet from Beaver Street. This is one of the lost thoroughfares of the city. Almost as old as the city itself, it once extended past the Fort and continued to the river in what is now Battery Place. It was then called Petticoat Lane. The first French Huguenot church was built on it in 1688. Now the Produce Exchange cuts the street off short and covers the site of the church.

Broad Street

Through Broad Street, when the town was New Amsterdam, a narrow, ill-smelling inlet extended to about the present Beaver Street, then narrowed to a ditch close to Wall Street. The waterfront was then at Pearl Street. Several bridges crossed the inlet, the largest at the point where Stone Street is. Another gave Bridge Street its name. In 1660 the ways on either side were paved, and soon became a market-place for citizens who traded with farmers for their products, and with the Indians who navigated the inlet in their canoes.

The locality has ever since been a centre of exchange. When the inlet was finally filled in it left the present "Broad" Street.

Where Beaver Street crosses this thoroughfare, on the northwest corner, is a tablet:

> TO COMMEMORATE THE GALLANT AND PATRIOTIC
> ACT OF MARINUS WILLIT IN HERE SEIZING
> JUNE, 6, 1775, FROM THE BRITISH FORCES THE
> MUSKETS WITH WHICH HE ARMED HIS
> TROOPS. THIS TABLE IS ERECTED BY
> THE SOCIETY OF THE SONS OF THE
> REVOLUTION, NEW YORK, NOV. 12, 1892

On one side of the tablet is a bas-relief of the scene showing the patriots stopping the ammunition wagons.

Fraunces Tavern

Fraunces Tavern, standing at the southeast corner of Broad and Pearl Streets, is much the same outwardly as it was when built in 1700, except that it has two added stories. Etienne De Lancey, a Huguenot nobleman, built it as his homestead and occupied it for a quarter of a century. It became a tavern under the direction of Samuel Fraunces in 1762. It was Washington's headquarters in 1776, and in 1783 he delivered there his farewell address to his generals.

Pearl Street

Pearl Street was one of the two early roads leading from the Fort. It lay along the water front, and extended to a ferry where Peck Slip is now. The road afterwards became Great Queen Street, and was lined with shops of store-keepers who sought the Long Island trade. The other road in time became Broadway.

On a building at 73 Pearl Street, facing Coenties Slip, is a tablet which reads:

THE SITE OF THE
FIRST DUTCH HOUSE OF ENTERTAINMENT
ON THE ISLAND OF MANHATTAN
LATER THE SITE OF THE OLD "STADT HUYS"
OR CITY HALL
THIS TABLE IS PLACED HERE BY
THE HOLLAND SOCIETY OF NEW YORK
SEPTEMBER, 1890

The First City Hall

This is the site of the first City Hall of New Amsterdam, built 1642. It stood by the waterside, for beyond Water Street all the land has been reclaimed. There was a court room and a prison in the building. Before it, where the pillars of the elevated road are now, was a cage and a whipping-post. There was also the public "Well of William Cox."

Beside the house ran a lane. It is there yet, still called Coenties Lane as in the days of old. But it is no longer green. Now it is narrow, paved, and almost lost between tall buildings.

Coenties Slip. The Miriam and Ira D. Wallach Division of Art, Prints and Photographs: Print Collection, NYPL Digital Collections, New York Public Library.

Opposite Coenties Lane is Coenties Slip, which was an inlet in the days of the Stadt Huys. The land about was owned by Conraet Ten Eyck, who was nicknamed Coentje. This in time became Coonchy and was finally vulgarized to "Quincy." The filling in of this waterway began in 1835 and the slip is now buried beneath Jeanette Park. The filled-in slip accounts for the width of the street. For the same reason there is considerable width at Wall, Maiden Lane and other streets leading to the water front.

First Printing Press in the Colony

At 81 Pearl Street, close by Coenties Slip, the first printing-press was set up by William Bradford, after he was appointed Public Printer in 1693. A tablet marks the site, with the inscription:

ON THIS SITE
WILLIAM BRADFORD
APPOINTED
PUBLIC PRINTER
APRIL 10, A.D. 1693
ESTABLISHED THE FIRST
PRINTING PRESS
IN THE
COLONY OF NEW YORK
ERECTED BY THE
NEW YORK
HISTORICAL SOCIETY
APRIL, 10, A. D. 1893
IN COMMEMORATION OF
THE 200TH ANNIVERSARY
OF THE INTRODUCTION
OF PRINTING IN
NEW YORK

Fire of 1835

Across the way, on a warehouse at 88 Pearl Street, is a marble tablet of unique design, to commemorate the great fire of 1835, which started in Merchant Street, burned for nineteen hours, extended over fifty acres and consumed 402 buildings.

Directly through the block from this point is Cuyler's Alley, a narrow way between the houses running off Water Street. Although it is a hundred years old the only incident connected with its existence that has crept into the city's history, is a murder. In 1823, a Boston merchant was waylaid and murdered for his money, and was dragged through this street for final disposition in the river, but the murderer made so much noise in his work that the constable heard him and came upon the abandoned corpse.

Stone Street

Through a pretty garden at the back of the Stadt Huys, Stone Street was reached. It was the first street to be laid with cobble-stones (1657), and so came by its name, which originally had been Brouwer Street.

Delmonico's establishment at Beaver and William Streets is on the site of the second of the Delmonico restaurants. (See Fulton and William Streets.)

Flat and Barrack Hill

Exchange Place took its name from the Merchants' Exchange, which was completed in William Street, fronting on Wall, in 1827 (the present Custom House). Before that date it had been called Garden Street. From Hanover to Broad Street was a famous place for boys to coast in winter, and the grade was called "Flat and Barrack Hill." Scarcely more than an alley now, the street was even narrower once and was given its present width in 1832.

Wall Street

Wall Street came by its name naturally, for it was a walled street once. When war broke out between England and Holland in 1653, Governor Peter Stuyvesant built the wall along the line of the present street, from river to river. His object was to form a barrier that should enclose the city. It was a wall of wood, twelve feet high, with a sloping breastwork inside. After the wall was removed in 1699, the street came to be a chief business thoroughfare.

Federal Hall

Federal Hall as it appeared in 1797. Library of Congress Prints and Photographs Division, Washington, DC.

A new City Hall, to replace the Stadt Huys, was built in 1699, at Nassau Street, on the site of the present Sub-Treasury building. In front of the building was the cage for criminals, stocks and whipping-post. When independence was declared, this building was converted into a capitol and was called Federal Hall. The Declaration of Independence was read from the steps in 1776. President Washington was inaugurated there in 1789. The wide strip of pavement on the west side of Nassau Street at Wall Street bears evidence of the former existence of Federal Hall. The latter extended across to the western house line of the present Nassau Street, and so closed the thoroughfare that a passage-way led around the building to Nassau Street.

When the Sub-Treasury was built in 1836, on the site of Federal Hall, Nassau Street was opened to Wall, and the little passage-way was left to form the wide pavement of to-day.

Where Alexander Hamilton Lived

Alexander Hamilton, in 1789, lived in a house on the south side of Wall Street at Broad. His slayer, Aaron Burr, then lived back of Federal Hall in Nassau Street.

The Custom House at William Street and Wall was completed in 1842. At this same corner once stood a statue of William Pitt, Earl of Chatham. In 1776, during the Revolution, the statue was pulled down by British soldiers, the head cut off and the remainder dragged in the mud. The people petitioned the Assembly in 1766 to erect the statue to Pitt, as a recognition of his zealous defence of the American colonies and his efforts in securing the repeal of the Stamp Act. At the same time provision was made for the erection of the equestrian statue of George III in Bowling Green. The statue of Pitt was of marble, and was erected in 1770.

Tontine Coffee House

The Tontine Building at the northwest corner of Wall and Water Streets marks the site of the Tontine Coffee House, a celebrated house for the interchange of goods and of ideas, and a political centre. It was a prominent institution in the city, resorted to by the wealthy and influential. The building was erected in 1794, and conducted by the Tontine Society of two hundred and three members, each holding a $200 share. Under their plan all property was to revert to seven survivors of the original subscribers. The division was made in 1876.

The Tontine Coffee House, Wall and Water Streets, about 1797. Library of Congress Prints and Photographs Division, Washington, DC.

Meal Market

Close to where the coffee house was built later, a market was set up in the middle of Wall Street in 1709, and being the public market for the sale of corn and meal was called the "Meal Market." Cut meat was not sold there until 1740. In 1731 this market became the only public place for the sale and hiring of slaves.

Trinity Church has stood at the head of Wall Street since 1697. Before 1779 the street was filled with tall trees, but during the intensely cold winter of that year most of them were cut down and used for kindling.

Birds-eye view of Trinity Church, New York, 1846. Library of Congress Prints and Photographs Division, Washington, DC.

The ferry wharf has been at the foot of the street since 1694, when the water came up as far as Pearl Street. It was here that Washington landed, coming from Elizabethport after his journey from Virginia, April 23, 1789, to be inaugurated.

The United States Hotel, Fulton, between Water and Pearl Streets, was built in 1823 as Holt's Hotel. It was the headquarters for captains of whaling ships and merchants. A semaphore, or marine telegraph, was on the cupola, the windmill-like arms of which served to indicate the arrival of vessels.

Middle Dutch Church

Middle Dutch Church, corner Nassau and Cedar Sts. The Miriam and Ira D. Wallach Division of Art, Prints and Photographs: Print Collection, NYPL Digital Collections.

On the building at the northeast corner of Nassau and Cedar Streets is a tablet reading:

HERE STOOD
THE MIDDLE DUTCH CHURCH
DEDICATED A. D. 1729
MADE A BRITISH MILITARY PRISON 1776
RESTORED 1790
OCCUPIED AS THE UNITED STATES POST-OFFICE
1845–1875
TAKEN DOWN 1882

This church was a notable place of worship; the last in the city to represent strict simplicity of religious service as contrasted with modern ease and elegance. The post-office occupied the building until its removal to the structure it now occupies. The second home of the Middle Dutch Church was in Lafayette Place.

Pie Woman's Lane

Nassau Street was opened in 1696, when Teunis de Kay was given the right to make a cartway from the wall to the commons (now City Hall Park). At first the street was known as Pie Woman's Lane.

The Maiden's Lane

Where Maiden Lane is there was once a narrow stream of spring water, which flowed from about the present Nassau Street. Women went there to wash their clothing, so that it came to be called the Virgin's Path, and from that the Maiden's Lane. A blacksmith having set up a shop at the edge of the stream near the river, the locality took the name of Smit's V'lei, or the Smith's Valley, afterwards shortened to the V'lei, and then readily corrupted to "Fly." It was natural, then, when a market was built on the Maiden's Lane, from Pearl to South Streets, to call it the Fly Market. This was pulled down in 1823.

The Jack-Knife

On Gold Street, northwest corner of Platt Street, is a wedge-shaped house of curious appearance. It is best seen from the Platt Street side. When this street was opened in 1834 by Jacob S. Platt, who owned much of the neighboring land and wanted a street of his own, the house was large and square and had been a tavern for a great many years. The new street cut the house to its present strange shape, and it came to be called the "Jack-knife."

Golden Hill

Golden Hill, celebrated since the time of the Dutch, is still to be seen in the high ground around Cliff and Gold Streets. Pearl Street near John shows a sweeping curve where it circled around the hill's base, and the same sort of curve is seen in Maiden Lane on the south and Fulton Street on the north. The first blood of the Revolution was shed on this hill in January, 1770, after the British soldiers had cut down a liberty pole set up by the Liberty Boys. The fight occurred on open ground back of an inn which still stands at 122 William Street, and is commemorated in a tablet on the wall of a building at the corner of John and William Streets. It reads:

"GOLDEN HILL"
HERE, JAN. 18, 1770
THE FIGHT TOOK PLACE BETWEEN THE
"SONS OF LIBERTY" AND THE
BRITISH REGULARS, 16TH FOOT
FIRST BLOODSHED IN THE
WAR OF THE REVOLUTION

The inn is much the same as in early days, except that many buildings crowd about it now, and modern paint has made it hideous to antiquarian eyes.

Golden Hill Inn

Delmonico's

On the east side of William Street, a few doors south of Fulton, John Delmonico opened a dingy little bake shop in 1823, acted as chef and waiter, and built up the name and business which to-day is synonymous with good eating. In 1832 he removed to 23 William Street. Burned out there in 1835, he soon opened on a larger scale with his brother at William and Beaver Streets, on which site is still an establishment under the Delmonico name. In time he set up various places—at Chambers Street and Broadway; Fourteenth Street and Fifth Avenue; Twenty-sixth Street and Broadway, and finally at Forty-fourth Street and Fifth Avenue.

John Street Church

John Street Church, between Nassau and William Streets, was the first Methodist Church in America. In 1767 it was organized in a loft at 120 William Street, then locally known as Horse and Cart Street. In 1768 the church was built in John Street. It was rebuilt in 1817 and again 1841. John Street perpetuates the name of John Harpendingh, who owned most of the land thereabout.

John Street Theatre

Interior of the John St. Theatre. The Miriam and Ira D. Wallach Division of Art, Prints and Photographs: Print Collection, NYPL Digital Collections.

At what is now 17, 19 and 21 John Street, in 1767 was built the old John Street Theatre, a wooden structure, painted red, standing sixty feet back from the street and reached by a covered way. An arcade through the house at No. 17 still bears evidence of the theatre. The house was closed in 1774, when the Continental Congress recommended suspension of amusements. Throughout the Revolutionary War, however, performances were given, the places of the players being filled by British officers. Washington frequently attended the performances at this theatre after he became President. The house was torn down in 1798.

Shakespeare Tavern

The site of the Shakespeare Tavern is marked by a tablet at the southwest corner of Nassau and Fulton Streets. The words of the tablet are:

ON THIS SITE IN THE
OLD SHAKESPEARE TAVERN
WAS ORGANIZED
THE SEVENTH REGIMENT
NATIONAL GUARD, S.N.Y.
AUG. 25, 1824

This tavern, low, old-fashioned, built of small yellow bricks with dormer windows in the roof, was constructed before the Revolution. In 1808 it was bought by Thomas Hodgkinson, an actor, and was henceforth a meeting-place for Thespians. It was resorted to—in contrast to the business men guests of the Tontine Coffee House—by the wits of the day, the poets and the writers. In 1824 Hodgkinson died, and the house was kept up for a time by his son-in-law; Mr. Stoneall.

First Clinton Hall

Mercantile Library Association, Clinton Hall. The Miriam and Ira D. Wallach Division of Art, Prints and Photographs: Print Collection, NYPL Digital Collections.

At the southwest corner of Beekman and Nassau Streets was built, in 1830, the first home of the Mercantile Library, called Clinton Hall. In 1820 the first steps were taken by the merchants of the city to establish a reading room for their clerks. The library was opened the following year with 700 volumes. In 1823 the association was incorporated. It was located first in a building in Nassau Street, but in 1826 was moved to Cliff Street, and in 1830 occupied its new building in Beekman Street. De Witt Clinton, Governor of the State, had presented a History of England as the first volume for the library. The new building was called Clinton Hall in his honor. In 1850, the building being crowded, the Astor Place Opera House was bought for $250,000, and remodeled in 1854 into the second Clinton Hall. The third building of that name is now on the site at the head of Lafayette Place.

St. George's Church

The St. George Building, on the north side of Beekman Street, just west of Cliff Street, stands on the site of St. George's Episcopal Church, a stately stone structure which was erected in 1811. In 1814 it was burned;

in 1816 rebuilt, and in 1845 removed to Rutherford Place and Sixteenth Street, where it still is. Next to the St. George Building is the tall shot-tower which may be so prominently seen from the windows of tall buildings in the lower part of the city, but is so difficult to find when search is made for it.

Barnum's Museum

P. T. Barnum, c. 1860–64. Library of Congress Prints and Photographs Division, Washington, DC.

Barnum's Museum, opened in 1842, was on the site of the St. Paul Building, at Broadway and Ann Street. There P. T. Barnum brought out Tom Thumb, the Woolly Horse and many other curiosities that became celebrated. On the stage of a dingy little amphitheatre in the house many actors played who afterwards won national recognition.

Original Park Theatre

The original Park Theatre was built in 1798, and stood on Park Row, between Ann and Beekman Streets, facing what was then City Hall Park and what is now the: Post Office. It was 200 feet from Ann Street, and extended back to the alley which has ever since been called Theatre Alley. John Howard Payne, author of "Home, Sweet Home," appeared there for the first time on any stage, in 1809, as the "Young American Roscius." In 1842 a ball in honor of Charles Dickens was given there. Many noted actors played at this theatre, which was the most important in the city at that period. It was rebuilt in 1820 and burned in 1848.

First Brick Presbyterian Church

At the junction of Park Row and Nassau Street, where the *Times* Building is, the Brick Presbyterian Church was erected in 1768. There was a small burying-ground within the shadow of its walls, and green fields stretched from it in all directions. It was sold in 1854, and a new church was built at Fifth Avenue and Thirty-seventh Street.

Where Leisler Was Hanged

Within a few steps of where the statue of Benjamin Franklin is in Printing House Square, Jacob Leisler was hanged in his own garden in 1691, the city's first martyr to constitutional liberty. A wealthy merchant, after James III fled and William III ascended the throne, Leisler was called by the Committee of Safety to act as Governor. He assembled a Continental Congress, whose deliberations were cut short by the arrival of Col. Henry Sloughter as Governor. Enemies of Leisler decided on his death. The new Governor refused to sign the warrant, but being made drunk signed it unknowingly and Leisler was hanged and his body buried at the foot of the scaffold. A few years later, a royal proclamation wiped the taint of treason from Leisler's memory and his body was removed to a more honored resting-place.

Tammany Hall

The walls of the *Sun* building at Park Row and Frankfort Street, are those of the first permanent home of Tammany Hall. Besides the hall it contained the second leading hotel in the city, where board was $7 a week. Tammany Hall, organized in 1789 by William Mooney, an upholsterer, occupied quarters in Borden's tavern in lower Broadway. In 1798 it removed to Martling's tavern, at the southeast corner of Nassau and Spruce, until its permanent home was erected in 1811.

A Liberty Pole

There is a tablet on the wall of the south corridor of the post-office building, which bears the inscription:

> ON THE COMMON OF THE CITY OF NEW YORK, NEAR WHERE THIS BUILDING NOW STANDS, THERE STOOD FROM 1766 TO 1776 A LIBERTY POLE ERECTED TO COMMEMORATE THE REPEAL OF THE STAMP ACT. IT WAS REPEATEDLY DESTROYED BY THE VIOLENCE OF THE TORIES AND AS REPEATEDLY REPLACED BY THE SONS OF LIBERTY, WHO ORGANIZED A CONSTANT WATCH AND GUARD. IN ITS DEFENCE THE FIRST MARTYR BLOOD OF THE AMERICAN REVOLUTION WAS SHED ON JAN. 18, 1770.

The cutting down of this pole led to the battle of Golden Hill.

City Hall Park

The post-office building was erected on a portion of the City Hall Park. This park, like all of the Island of Manhattan, was a wilderness a few hundred years ago. By 1661, where the park is there was a clearing in which cattle were herded. In time the clearing was called The Fields; later The Commons. On The Commons, in Dutch colonial days, criminals were executed.

Potter's Field In City Hall Park

Still later a Potter's field occupied what is now the upper end of the Park; above it, and extending over the present Chambers Street was a negro burying-ground. On these commons, in 1735, a poor-house was built, the site of which is covered by the present City Hall. From time to time other buildings were erected.

The new Jail was finished in 1763, and, having undergone but few alterations, is now known as the Hall of Records. It was a military prison during the Revolution, and afterwards a Debtors' Prison. In 1830 it became the Register's Office. It was long considered the most beautiful building in the city, being patterned after the temple of Diana of Ephesus.

The Bridewell, or City Prison, was built on The Commons in 1775, close by Broadway, on a line with the Debtors' Prison. It was torn down in 1838.

Cell in the Prison
under the Hall of Records

Third City Hall

The present City Hall was finished in 1812. About that time The Commons were fenced in and became a park, taking in besides the present space, that now occupied by the post office building. The constructors of the City Hall deemed it unnecessary to use marble for the rear wall as they had for the sides and front, and built this wall of freestone, it being then almost inconceivable that traffic could ever extend so far up-town as to permit a view of the rear of the building.

Governor's Room

The most noted spot in the City Hall is the Governor's Room, an apartment originally intended for the use of the Governor when in the city. In time it became the municipal portrait gallery, and a reception room for the distinguished guests of the city. The bodies of Abraham Lincoln and of John Howard Payne lay in state in this room. With it is also associated the visit of Lafayette when he returned to this country in 1824 and made reception headquarters. The room was also the scene of the celebration after the capture of the "Guerrière" by the "Constitution"; the reception to Commodore Perry after his Lake Erie victory; the celebration in connection with the laying of the Atlantic cable; and at the completion of the Erie Canal. It contains a large gilt punch-bowl, showing scenes in New York a hundred years ago. This was presented to the city by General Jacob Morton, Secretary of the Committee of Defense, at the opening of the City Hall.

At the western end of the front wall of City Hall is a tablet reading:

NEAR THE SPOT IN THE PRESENCE OF
GEN. GEORGE WASHINGTON
THE DECLARATION OF
INDEPENDENCE
WAS READ AND PUBLISHED
TO THE
AMERICAN ARMY
JULY 9TH, 1776

First Savings Bank

Other buildings erected in the Park First were The Rotunda, 1816, on the site of the brown stone building afterwards occupied by the Court of General Sessions, where works of art were exhibited; and the New York Institute on the site of the Court House, occupied in 1817 by the American, or Scudder's Museum, the first in the city. The Chambers Street Bank, the first bank for savings in the city, opened in the basement of the Institute building in 1818. In 1841 Philip Hone was president of this bank. It afterwards moved to the north side of Bleecker Street, between Broadway and

Crosby, and became the Bleecker Street Bank. Now it is at Twenty-second Street and Fourth Avenue, and is called The Bank for Savings.

The statue of Nathan Hale was erected in City Hall Park by the Sons of the Revolution. Some authorities still insist that the Martyr Spy was hanged in this park.

Fences of City Hall Park

Until 1821 there were fences of wooden pickets about the park. In that year iron railings, which had been imported from England, were set up, with four marble pillars at the southern entrance. The next year trees were set out within the enclosure, and just within the railing were planted a number of rose-bushes which had been supplied by two ladies who had an eye to landscape gardening. Frosts and vandals did not allow the bushes more than a year of life. Four granite balls, said to have been dug from the ruins of Troy, were placed on the pillars at the southern entrance, May 8, 1827. They were given to the city by Captain John B. Nicholson, U. S. N.

The building 39 and 41 Chambers Street, opposite the Court House, stands on the site of the pretty little Palmo Opera House, built in 1844 for the production of Italian opera, by F. Palmo, the wealthy proprietor of the Café des Mille Colonnes on Broadway at Duane Street. He lost his fortune in the operatic venture and became a bartender. In 1848 the house became Burton's Theatre. About 1800, this site was occupied by the First Reformed Presbyterian Church, a frame building which was replaced by a brick structure in 1818. The church was moved to Prince and Marion Streets in 1834.

Office of Aaron Burr

At No. 11 Reade Street is a dingy little house, now covered with signs and given over to half a dozen small business concerns, about which hover memories of Aaron Burr. It was here he had a law office in 1832, and here when he was seventy-eight years old he first met Mme. Jumel whom he afterwards married. The house is to be torn down to make way for new municipal buildings.

An Historic Window

At Rose and Duane Streets stands the Rhinelander building, and on the Rose Street side close by the main entrance is a small grated window. This is the last trace of a sugar-house, which, during the Revolutionary War, was used as a British military prison. The building was not demolished until 1892, and the window, retaining its original position in the old house, was built into the new.

The Tombs Prison

Where the Tombs prison stands was once the Collect, or Fresh Water Pond. This deep body of water took up, approximately, the space between the present Baxter, Elm, Canal and Pearl Streets. When the Island of Manhattan was first inhabited, a swamp stretched in a wide belt across it from where Roosevelt Slip is now to the end of Canal Street on the west side. The Collect was the centre of this stretch, with a stream called the Wreck Brook flowing from it across a marsh to the East River.

"The Tombs"

The Collect

At a time near the close of the eighteenth century a drain was cut from the Collect to the north River, on a line with the present Canal Street. With the progress of the city to the north, the pond was drained, and the swamp made into firm ground. In 1816, the Corporation Yards occupied the block of Elm, Centre, Leonard and Franklin Streets, on the ground which had filled in the pond. The Tombs, or City Prison, was built on this block in 1838.

The Five Points

The Five Points still exists where Worth, Baxter and Park Streets intersect, but it is no longer the centre of a community of crime that gained international notoriety. It was once the gathering-point for criminals and degraded persons of both sexes and of all nationalities, a rookery for thieves and murderers. Its history began more than a century and a half ago. During the so-called Negro Insurrection of 1741, when many negroes were hanged, the severest punishment was the burning at the stake of fourteen negroes m this locality.

Mulberry Bend Slum

One of the five "Points" is now formed by a pleasant park which a few years ago took the place of the last remnant of the old-time locality. In no single block of the city was there ever such a record for crime as in this old "Mulberry Bend" block. Set low in a hollow, it was a refuge for the outcasts of the city and of half a dozen countries. The slum took its name, as the park does now, from Mulberry Street, which on one side of it makes a deep and sudden bend. In this slum block the houses were three deep in places, with scarcely the suggestion of a courtyard between them. Narrow alleys, hardly wide enough to permit the passage of a man, led between houses to beer cellars, stables and time-blackened, tumbledown tenements. Obscure ways honeycombed the entire block—ways that led beneath houses, over low sheds, through fragments of wall—ways that were known only to the thief and the tramp. There "Bottle Alley," "Bandit's Roost" and "Ragpicker's Row" were the scenes of many wild fights, and many a time the ready stiletto ended the lives of men, or the heavy club dashed out brains.

The Five Points House of Industry's work was begun in 1850, and has been successful in ameliorating the moral and physical condition of the people of the vicinity. The institution devoted to this work stands on the site of the "Old Brewery," the most notorious criminal resort of the locality.

An Ancient Church

At Mott and Park Streets is now the Church of the Transfiguration (Catholic). On a hill, the suggestion of which is still to be seen in steep Park Street, the Zion Lutheran Church was erected in 1797. In 1810 it was changed to Zion Episcopal Church. It was burned in 1815, rebuilt 1819, and sold in 1853 to the Church of the Transfiguration, which has occupied it since. This last church had previously been in Chambers Street, and before that it had occupied several quarters. It was founded in 1827, and is the fourth oldest church in the diocese. Zion Episcopal Church moved in 1853 to Thirty-eighth Street and Madison Avenue, and in 1891 consolidated with St. Timothy's Church at No. 332 West Fifty-seventh Street. The Madison Avenue building was sold to the South (Reformed) Dutch Church.

PARK St. with
CHURCH of the TRANSFIGURATION

Chatham Square

Chatham Square has been the open space it is now ever since the time when a few houses clustered about Fort Amsterdam. The road that stretched the length of the island in 1647 formed the only connecting link between the fort and six large bouweries or farms on the east side.

The bouwerie settlers in the early days were harassed by Indians, and spent as much time defending themselves and skurrying off to the protection of the Fort as they did in improving the land. The earliest settlement in the direction of these bouweries, which had even a suggestion of permanency, was on a hill which had once been an Indian outlook, close by the present Chatham Square. Emanuel de Groot, a giant negro, with ten superannuated slaves, were permitted to settle here upon agreeing to pay each a fat hog and 22 1/2 bushels of grain a year, their children to remain slaves.

Bouwerie Lane

North of this settlement stretched a primeval forest through which cattle wandered and were lost. Then the future Chatham Square was fenced in as a place of protection for the cattle.

The lane leading from this enclosure to the outlying bouweries, during the Revolution was used for the passage of both armies. At that period the highway changed from the Bouwerie Lane of the Dutch to the English Bowery Road. In 1807 it became "The Bowery."

Kissing Bridge

The Kissing Bridge. The Miriam and Ira D. Wallach Division of Art, Prints and Photographs: Print Collection, NYPL Digital Collections.

The earliest "Kissing Bridge" was over a small creek, on the Post Road, close by the present Chatham Square. Travelers who left the city by this road parted with their friends on this bridge, it being the custom to accompany the traveler thus far from the city on his way.

What is now Park Row, from City Hall Park to Chatham Square, was for many years called Chatham Street, in honor of William Pitt, Earl of Chatham. In 1886 the aldermen of the city changed the name to Park Row, and in so doing seemed to stamp approval of an event just one hundred years before which had stirred American manhood to acts of valor. This was the dragging down by British soldiers in 1776 of a statue of the Earl of Chatham which had stood in Wall Street.

Tea Water Pump

The most celebrated pump in the city was the Tea Water Pump, on Chatham Street (now Park Row) near Queen (now Pearl) Street. The water was supplied from the Collect and was considered of the rarest quality for the making of tea. Up to 1789 it was the chief water-works of the city, and the water was carted about the city in casks and sold from carts.

Home of Charlotte Temple

Within a few steps of the Bowery, on the north side of Pell Street, in a frame house, Charlotte Temple died. The heroine of Mrs. Rawson's "Tale of Truth," whose sorrowful life was held up as a moral lesson a generation ago, had lived first in a house on what is now the south side of Astor Place close to Fourth Avenue. Her tomb is in Trinity churchyard.

Bull's Head Tavern

The Bull's Head Tavern was built on the site of the present Thalia Theatre, formerly the Bowery Theatre, just above Chatham Square, some years before 1763. It was frequented by drovers and butchers, and was the most popular tavern of its kind in the city for many years. Washington and his staff occupied it on the day the British evacuated the city in 1783. It was pulled down in 1826, making way for the Bowery Theatre,

First Bowery Theatre

The Bowery Theatre was opened in 1826, and during the course of its existence was the home of broad melodrama, that had such a large following that the theatre obtained a national reputation. Many celebrated actors appeared in the house. It was burned in 1828, rebuilt and burned again in 1836, again in 1838, in 1845 and in 1848.

New Bowery Street was opened from the south side of Chatham Square in 1856. The street carried away a part of a Jewish burying-ground, a portion of which, crowded between tenement-houses and shut off from the street by a wall and iron fence, is still to be seen a few steps from Chatham Square. The first synagogue of the Jews was in Mill Street (now

South William). The graveyard mentioned was the first one used by this congregation, and was opened in 1681, so far from the city that it did not seem probable that the latter could ever reach it. Early in the nineteenth century the graveyard was moved to a site which is now Sixth Avenue and Eleventh Street.

Washington's Home on Cherry Hill

The Franklin House was the first place of residence of George Washington in the city, when he became President in 1789. It stood at the corner of Franklin Square (then St. George Square) and Cherry Street. A portion of the East River Bridge structure rests on the site. Pearl Street, passing the house, was a main thoroughfare in those days. The house was built in 1770 by Walter Franklin, an importing merchant. It was torn down in 1856. The site is marked by a tablet on the Bridge abutment, which reads:

THE FIRST
PRESIDENTIAL MANSION
NO. 1 CHERRY STREET
OCCUPIED BY
GEORGE WASHINGTON
FROM APRIL 23, 1789
TO FEBRUARY 23, 1790
ERECTED BY THE
MARY WASHINGTON COLONIAL CHAPTER, D. A. R.
APRIL 30, 1899

At No.7 Cherry Street gas was first introduced into the city in 1825. This is the Cherry Hill district, sadly deteriorated from the merry days of its infancy. Its name is still preserved in Cherry Street, which is hemmed in by tenement-houses which the Italian population crowd in almost inconceivable numbers. At the top of the hill, where these Italians drag out a crowded existence, Richard Sackett, an Englishman, established a pleasure garden beyond the city in 1670, and because its chief attraction was an orchard of cherry trees, called it the Cherry Garden—a name that has since clung to the locality.

II

The Origin of Broadway

From New Amsterdam, which centered about the Fort, the only road which led through the island branched out from Bowling Green. It took the line of what is now Broadway, and during a period of one hundred years was the only road which extended the length of the island.

That Broadway, beyond St. Paul's Chapel, ever became a greatly traveled thoroughfare, was due more to accident than design, for to all appearances the road which turned to the east was to be the main artery for the city's travel, and all calculations were made to that end. Broadway really ended at St. Paul's.

The First Graveyard

Morris Street was called Beaver Lane before the name was changed in 1829. On this street, near Broadway, the first graveyard of the city was situated. It was removed and the ground sold at auction in 1676, when a plot was acquired opposite Wall Street. This last was used in conjunction with Trinity Church until city interment was prohibited.

The First House Built

On the office building at 41 Broadway there is fixed a tablet which bears the inscription:

> THIS TABLET MARKS THE SITE OF THE
> FIRST HABITATIONS OF WHITE MEN
> ON THE ISLAND OF MANHATTAN
> ADRIAN BLOCK
> COMMANDER OF THE "TIGER"
> ERECTED HERE FOUR HOUSES OR HUTS
> AFTER HIS VESSEL WAS BURNED
> NOVEMBER 1613
> HE BUILT THE RESTLESS, THE FIRST VESSEL
> MADE BY EUROPEANS IN THIS COUNTRY
> THE RESTLESS WAS LAUNCHED
> IN THE SPRING OF 1614

Adrian Block was one of the earliest fur traders to visit the island after Henry Hudson returned to Holland with the news of his discovery. The "Tiger "took fire in the night while anchored in the bay, and Block and his crew reached the shore with difficulty. They were the only white men on the island. Immediately they set about building a new vessel, which was named the "Restless."

Next door, at No. 39, President Washington lived in the Macomb's Mansion, moving there from the Franklin House in 1790. Subsequently the house became a hotel.

Tin Pot Alley

There is a rift in the walls between the tall buildings at No. 55 Broadway, near Rector Street, a cemented way that is neither alley nor street. It was a green lane before New Amsterdam became New York, and for a hundred years has been called Tin Pot Alley. With the growth of the city the little lane came near being crowded out, and the name, not being of proper dignity, would be forgotten but for a terra cotta tablet fixed in a building at its entrance. This was placed there by Rev. Morgan Dix, the pastor of Trinity Church.

At the southwest corner of Broadway and Rector Street, where a skyscraper is now, Grace Church once stood with a graveyard about it. The church was completed in 1808, and was there until 1846, when the present structure was erected at Broadway and Tenth Street. Upon the Rector Street site, the Trinity Lutheran Church, a log structure, was built in 1671, It was rebuilt in 1741, and was burned in the great fire of 1776.

Trinity Churchyard

Trinity churchyard is part of a large tract of land, granted to the Trinity Corporation in 1705, that was once the Queen's Farm.

In 1635 there were a number of bouweries or farms above the Fort. The nearest—one extending about to where Warren Street is—was set apart for the Dutch West India Company, and called the Company's Farm. Above this was another, bounded approximately by what are now Warren and Charlton Streets, west of Broadway. This last was given by the company, in 1635, to Roelof Jansz (contraction of Jannsen), a Dutch colonist. He died the following year, and the farm became the property of his wife, Annetje Jans. (In the feminine, the z being omitted, the form became Jans.) The farm was sold to Francis Lovelace, the English Governor, in 1670, and he added it to the company's farm, and it became thereafter the Duke's Farm. In 1674 it became the King's Farm. When Queen Anne began her reign it became the Queen's Farm, and it was she who granted it to Trinity, making it the Church Farm.

Annetje Jans's Farm

In 1731, which was sixty-one years after the Annetje Jans's farm was sold to Governor Lovelace, the descendants of Annetje Jans for the first time decided that they had yet some interest in the farm, and made an unsuccessful protest. From time to time since protests in the form of lawsuits have been made, but no court has sustained the claims. The city's growth was retarded by church ownership of land, as no one wanted to build on leasehold property. It was not until the greater part of available land on the east side of the island was built upon that the church property was made use of on the only terms it could be had. Not until 1803 were the streets from Warren to Canal laid out.

Trinity Church was built in 1697. For years before, however, there had been a burying-ground beyond the city and the city's wall that became the Trinity graveyard of to-day. The waving grass extended to a bold bluff overlooking Hudson River, which was about where Greenwich Street now is. Through the bluff a street was cut, its passage being still plainly to be seen in the high wall on the Trinity Place side of the graveyard.

Oldest Grave In Trinity Churchyard

The oldest grave of which there is a record is in the northern section of the churchyard, on the left of the first path. It is that of a child, and is marked with a sandstone slab, with a skull, crossbones and winged hour-glass cut in relief on the back, the inscription on the front reading:

W. C.
HEAR . LYES . THE . BODY
OF . RICHARD . CHVRCH
ER . SON . OF . WILLIA
M. CHVRCHER . WHO .
DIED . THE . 5 OF . APRIL
1681 . OF . AGE 5 YEARS
AND . 5 . MONTHS

The records tell nothing of the Churcher family.

Within a few feet of this stone is another that countless eves have looked at through the iron fence from Broadway, which says:

HA, SYDNEY, SYDNEY!
LYEST THOU HERE?
I HERE LYE,
'TIL TIME IS FLOWN
TO ITS EXTREMITY.

It is the grave of a merchant—once an officer of the British army—Sydney Breese, who wrote his epitaph and directed that it be placed on his tombstone. He died in 1767.

Grave of Charlotte Temple

On the opposite side of the path, nearer to Broadway, is a marble slab lying flat on the ground and each year sinking deeper into the earth. It was placed there by one of the sextons of Trinity more than a century ago, in memory of Charlotte Temple.

Close by the porch of the north entrance to the church is the stone that marks the grave of William Bradford, who set up the first printing-press in the colony and was printer to the Colonial Government for fifty years. He was ninety-two years old when he died in 1752. The original stone was crumbling to decay when, in 1863, the Vestry of Trinity Church replaced it by the present stone, renewing the original inscription.

Martyrs' Monument

The tall freestone Gothic shaft, the only monumental pile in the northern section of the churchyard, serves to commemorate the unknown dead of the Revolution. Trinity Church with all its records, together with a large section of the western part of the city, was burned in 1776 when the British army occupied the city. During the next seven years the only burials in the graveyard were the American prisoners from the Provost Jail in The Commons and the other crowded prisons of the city, who were interred at night and without ceremony. No record was kept of who the dead were.

A Churchyard Cryptograph

Close to the Martyrs' Monument is a stone so near the fence that its inscription can be read from Broadway:

HERE LIES
DEPOSITED THE BODY OF
JAMES LEESON,
WHO DEPARTED THIS LIFE ON
THE 28TH DAY OF SEPTEMBER, 1794,
AGED 38 YEARS.

And above the inscription are cut these curious characters :

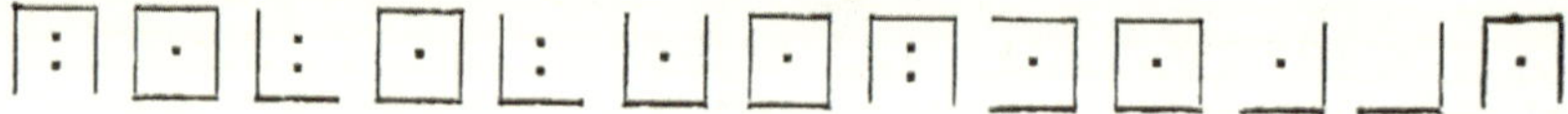

It is a cryptograph, but a simple one, familiar to school children. In its solution three diagrams are drawn and lettered thus:

A	B	C
D	E	F
G	H	I

K	L	M
N	O	P
Q	R	S

T	U	V
W	X	Y
Z		

The lines which enclose the letters are separated from the design, and each section used instead of the letters. For example, the letters A, B, C, become :

The second series begins with K, because the I sign is also used for J. The letters of the three series are distinguished by dots; one dot being placed with the lines of the first series; two dots with the second, but none with the third. If this be tried, any one can readily decipher the meaning of the cryptograph, and read "REMEMBER DEATH."

Close to the north door of the church are interred the remains of Lady Cornbury, who could call England's Queen Anne cousin. She was the wife of Edward Hyde, Lord Cornbury, who was Governor of New York in 1702. He was a grandson of the Earl of Clarendon, Prime Minister of Charles II; and son of that Earl of Clarendon who was brother-in-law of James II. So Lady Cornbury was first cousin of Queen Anne. She was Baroness of Clifton in her own right, and a gracious lady. She died in 1706.

Alexander Hamilton's Tomb

The tomb of Alexander Hamilton, patriot, soldier and statesman, stands conspicuously in the southern half of the churchyard, about forty feet from Broadway and ten feet from the iron railing on Rector Street.

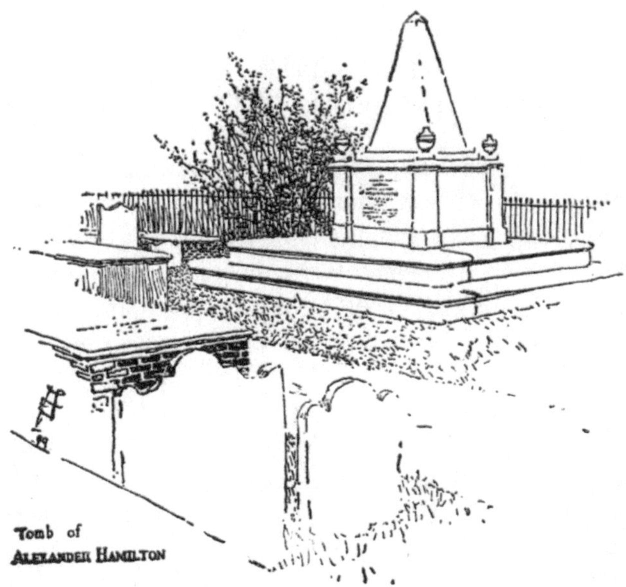

Tomb of
ALEXANDER HAMILTON

In the same part of the churchyard are interred the remains of Philip, eldest son of Alexander Hamilton. The son in 1801 fell in a duel with George L. Eacker, a young lawyer, when the two disagreed over a political matter. Three years later Eacker died and was buried in St. Paul's churchyard, and the same year Alexander Hamilton fell before the duelling pistol of Aaron Burr.

Last Friend of Aaron Burr

Close by Hamilton's tomb, a slab almost buried in the earth bears the inscription "Matthew L. Davis' Sepulchre." Strange that this "last friend that Aaron Burr possessed on earth" should rest in death so close to his friend's great enemy. He went to the Jersey shore in a row-boat with Burr on the day the duel was fought with Hamilton, and stood not far away with Dr. Hosack to await the outcome. He was imprisoned for refusing to testify before the Coroner. Afterwards he wrote a life of Burr. He was a merchant, with a store at 49 Stone Street, and was highly respected.

Tomb of Capt. James Lawrence

Within a few steps of Broadway, at the southern entrance to the church, is the tomb of Captain James Lawrence, U.S.N., who was killed on board the frigate Chesapeake during the engagement with H.B.M. frigate "Shannon." His dying words, "Don't give up the ship!" are now known to every schoolboy. The handsome mausoleum close by the church door, and the surrounding eight cannon, first attract the eye. These cannon, selected from arms captured from the English in the war of 1812, are buried deep, according to the directions of the Vestry of Trinity, in order that the national insignia, and the inscription telling of the place and time of capture, might be hidden and no evidence of triumph paraded in that place--where all are equal, where peace reigns and enmity is unknown. The monument was erected August 22, 1844. Before that the remains of Captain Lawrence had been interred in the southwest corner of the churchyard, beneath a shaft of white marble. This first resting-place was selected in September, 1813, when the body was brought to the city and interred, after being carried m funeral procession from the Battery.

"D. Contant" is the inscription on the first vault at the south entrance, one of the first victims of the revocation of the Edict of Nantes to be buried in the city. There are many Huguenot memorials in the churchyard, the oddest being a tombstone with a Latin inscription telling that Withamus de Marisco, who died in 1765, was "most noble on the side of his father's mother."

Cresap, the Indian Fighter

At the rear of the church, to the north, is a small headstone:

IN MEMORY OF
MICHAEL CRESAP
FIRST CAPTAIN OF THE
RIFLE BATTALIONS
AND SON OF COLONEL THOMAS CRESAP
WHO DEPARTED THIS LIFE
OCT. 18, A. D, 1775.

His father had been a friend and neighbor of Washington in Virginia, and he himself was a brilliant Indian fighter on the frontier of his native State. It was the men under his command who, unordered, exterminated the family of Logan, the Indian chief, "the friend of the white man." Many a boy, who in school declaimed, unthinkingly, "Who is there to mourn for Logan? Not one!" grown to manhood, cannot but look with interest on the grave of Logan's foe. Tradition has been kind to Cresap's memory, insisting that his heart broke over the accusation of responsibility for the death of Logan's family.

There is another slab, close by the grave of Captain Cresap, which tells:

> "HERE LIETH YE BODY OF SUSANNAH NEAN, WIFE OF ELIAS NEAN, BORN IN YE CITY OF ROCHELLE, IN FRANCE, IN YE YEAR 1660, WHO DEPARTED THIS LIFE 25 DAY OF DECEMBER, 1720, AGE 60 YEARS." "HERE LIETH ENTERREO YE BODY OF ELIAS NEAN, CATECHIST IN NEW YORK, BORN IN SOUBISE, IN YE PROVINCE OF CAENTONGE IN FRANCE IN YE YEAR 1662, WHO DEPARTED THIS LIFE 8 DAY OF SEPTEMBER 1722 AGED 60 YEARS." "THIS INSCRIPTION WAS RESTORED BY ORDER OF THEIR DESCENDANT OF

THE 6TH GENERATION, ELIZABETH CHAMPLIN PERRY, WIDOW OF THE LATE COM'R O. H. PERRY, OF THE U. S. NAVY, MAY, ANNO DOMINI, 1846."

But the stone does not tell that the Huguenot refugee was for many years a vestryman of Trinity Church, and that among his descendants are the Belmonts and a dozen distinguished families. Before coming to America, Elias Nean can was condemned to the galleys in France because he refused to renounce the reformed religion.

Where Gov. De Lancey Was Buried

Beneath the middle aisle in the church lie the bones of the eldest son of Stephen (Etienne) De Lancey--James De Lancey. He was Chief Justice of the Colony of New York in 1733, and Lieutenant Governor in 1753. He died suddenly in 1760 at his country house which was at the present northwest corner of Delancey and Chrystie Streets. A lane led from the house to the Bowery.

Home of the De Lanceys

Thames Street is as narrow now as it was one hundred and fifty years ago, when it was a carriageway that led to the stables of Etienne De Lancey. The Huguenot nobleman left his Broad Street house for the new home he had built at Broadway and Cedar Street in 1730. In 1741, at his death, it became the property of his son, James, the Lieutenant-Governor. It was the most imposing house in the town, elegantly decorated, encircled by broad balconies, with an uninterrupted garden extending to the river at the back.

After the death of Lieutenant-Governor De Lancey in 1760, the house became a hotel, and was known under many names. It was a favorite place for British officers during the Revolution, and in 1789 was the scene of the first "inauguration ball" in honor of President Washington.

The house was torn down in 1793. In 1806 the City Hotel was erected on its site and became the most fashionable in town. It was removed in 1850 and a line of shops set up. In 1889 the present buildings were erected.

A tablet on the building at 113 Broadway, corner of Cedar Street, marks the site, reading:

THE SITE OF
LIEUT. GOVE. DE LANCEY'S HOUSE ·
LATER THE CITY HOTEL.
IT WAS HERE THAT THE NON-IMPORTATOIN
AGREEMENT, IN OPPOSITION TO THE STAMPE
ACT, WAS SIGNED, OCT. 15TH, 1766. THE
TAVERN HAD MANY PROPRIETORS BY WHOSE
NAMES IT WAS SUCCESSIVELY CALLED. IT
WAS ALSO KNOWN AS THE PROVINCE ARMS, THE
CITY ARMS AND BURNS COFFEE HOUSE OR TAVERN.

Opposite Liberty (then Crown) Street, at the centre of Broadway, there stood in 1789 a detached building 42 X 25 feet. It was the" up-town market," patronized by the wealthy, who did their own marketing in those days, their black slaves carrying the purchases home.

Washington Market

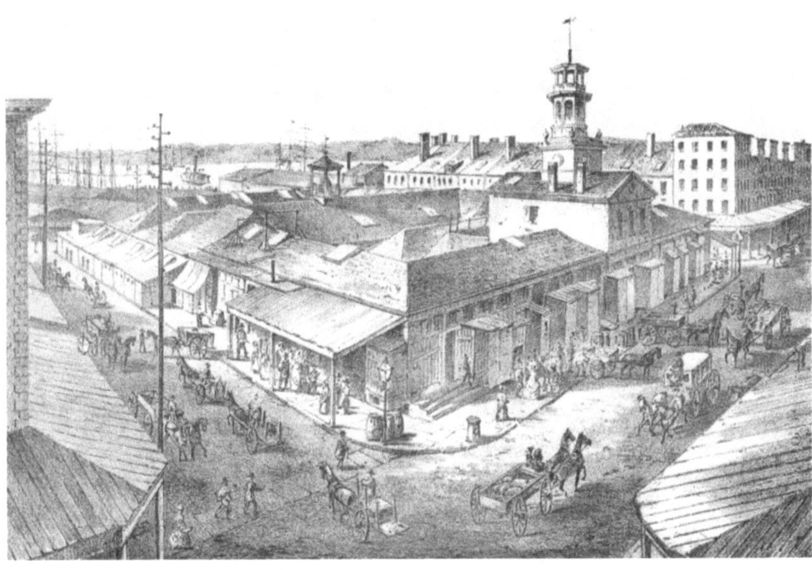

Washington Market from the S. E. corner of Fulton and Market Streets, 1859. The Miriam and Ira D. Wallach Division of Art, Prints and Photographs: Print Collection, NYPL Digital Collections.

Washington Market, at the foot of Fulton Street, was built in 1833. The water washed the western side of it then, and ships sailed to it to deliver their freight. Since then the water has been crowded back year by year with the growing demand for land. In its early days it was variously called Country Market, Fish Market and Exterior Market.

St. Paul's Chapel

St. Paul's Chapel and the Astor Hotel, viewed from Broadway. The Miriam and Ira D. Wallach Division of Art, Prints and Photographs: Print Collection, NYPL Digital Collections.

At the outskirts of the city, in a field that the same year had been sown with wheat, the cornerstone of St. Paul's Chapel was laid on May 14, 1764. The church was opened two years later, and the steeple added in 1794. It fronted the river which came up then as far as to where Greenwich Street is now, and a grassy lawn sloped down to a beach of pebbles. During the days of English occupancy, Major Andre, Lord Howe and Sir Guy Carleton worshipped there. Another who attended services there was the English midshipman who afterwards became William IV.

The Washington Pew in St. Paul's

President Washington, on the day of his inauguration, marched at the head of the representative men of the new nation to attend service in St. Paul's, and thereafter attended regularly. The pew he occupied has been presented and is still to be seen next the north wall, midway between the chancel and the vestry room. Directly opposite is the pew occupied at the same period by Governor George Clinton.

Waſhington Pew
St PAUL'S CHAPEL

Back of the chancel is the monument to Major-General Richard Montgomery, who fell before Quebec in 1775, crying, "Men of New York, you will not fail to follow where your general leads!" Congress decided on the monument, and Benjamin Franklin bought it in France for 300 guineas. A privateer bringing it to this country was captured by a British gunboat, which in turn was taken, and the monument, arriving safe here, was set in place. The body was removed from its first resting-place in Quebec, and interred close beside the monument in 1818.

In the burying-ground, which has been beside the church since it was built, are the monuments of men whose names are associated with the city's history : Dr. William James Macneven, who raised chemistry to a science; Thomas Addis Emmet, an eminent jurist and brother of Robert Emmet; Christopher Collis, who established the first water works in the city, and who first conceived the idea of constructing the Erie Canal; and a host of others.

The Actor Cooke's Grave

The tomb of George Frederick Cooke, the tragedian, is conspicuous m the centre of the yard, facing the main door of the church. Cooke was born in England in 1756, and died in New York in 1811. Early in life he was a printer's apprentice. By 1800 he had taken high rank among tragic actors.

The grave of George L. Eacker, who killed the eldest son of Alexander Hamilton in a duel, is near the Vesey Street railing.

Astor House

The Astor House, occupying the Broadway block between Vesey and Barclay Streets, was opened in 1836 by Boyden, a hotel keeper of Boston. This site had been part of the Church Farm, and as early as 1719, when there were only a few scattered farm houses on the island above what is now Liberty Street, there was a farm house on the Astor House site; and from there extended, on the Broadway line, a ropewalk. Prior to the erection of the hotel in 1830, the site for the most part had been occupied by the homes of John Jacob Astor, John G. Coster and David Lydig. On a part of the site, at 221 Broadway, in 1817, M. Paff, popularly known as "Old Paff," kept a bric-à-brac store. He dealt especially in paintings, having the reputation of buying worthless and old ones and "restoring" them into masterpieces. His was the noted curiosity-shop of the period.

A House of Other Days

Where Vesey and Greenwich Streets and West Broadway come together is a low, rough-hewn rock house. It has been used as a shoe store since the early part of the century. On its roof is a monster boot bearing the date of 1831, which took part in the Croton water parade and a dozen other celebrations. In pre-revolutionary days, when the ground where the building stands was all Hudson River, and the water extended as far as the present Greenwich Street, according to tradition, this was a lighthouse. There have been many changes in the outward appearance, but the foundation of solid rock is the same as when the waters swept around it.

The Road to Greenwich

Greenwich Street follows the line of a road which led from the city to Greenwich Village. This road was on the waterside. It was called Greenwich Road. South of Canal Street, west of Broadway, was a marshy tract known as Lispenard's Meadows. Over this swamp Greenwich Road crossed on a raised causeway. When the weather was bad for any length of time, the road became so heavy and in places was covered by the strong tide from the river. At such times travel took an inland route, along the Post Road (now the Bowery) and by Obelisk Lane (now Astor Place and Greenwich Avenue).

St. Peter's Church

St. Peter's Church, at the southeast corner of Barclay and Church Streets, the home of the oldest Roman Catholic congregation in the city, was built in 1786, and rebuilt in 1838. The congregation was formed in 1783, although mass was celebrated in private houses before that for the few scattered Catholic families.

Columbia College

The two blocks included between Barclay and Murray Streets, West Broadway and Church Street, were occupied until 1857 by the buildings and grounds of Columbia College. That part of the Queen's Far lying west of Broadway between the present Barclay and Murray Streets--a strip of land then in the outskirts of the city—in 1754 was given to the governors of King's College. During the Revolution the college suspended exercises, resuming in 1784 as Columbia College under an act passed by the Legislature of the State. In 1814, in consideration of lands before granted to the college which had been ceded to New Hampshire in settlement of the boundary, the college was granted by the State a tract of farming land known as the Hosack Botanical Garden. This is the twenty acres lying between Forty-seventh and Forty-ninth Streets, Fifth and Sixth Avenues. At that time the city extended but little above the City Hall Park, and this land was unprofitable and for many years of considerable expense to the college. By 1839 the city had crept past the college and the locality being built up the college grounds were cramped between the limits of two blocks. In 1854, Park Place was opened through the grounds of the college from Church Street to West Broadway (then called College Place). Until about 1816 the section of Park Place west of the college grounds was called Robinson Street. In 1857 the college was moved to Madison Avenue, between Forty-ninth and Fiftieth Streets, and in 1890 it was re-organized on a university basis.

Chapel Place

West Broadway was originally a lane which wound from far away Canal Street to the Chapel of Columbia College, and was called Chapel Place. Later it became College Place. In 1892 the street was widened south of Chambers Street, in order to relieve the great traffic from the north, and extended through the block from Barclay to Greenwich Street. Evidence of the former existence of the old street can be seen in the pillars of the elevated road on the west side of West Broadway at Murray Street, for these pillars, once on the sidewalk, are now several feet from it in the street.

Bowling Green Garden and First Vauxhall

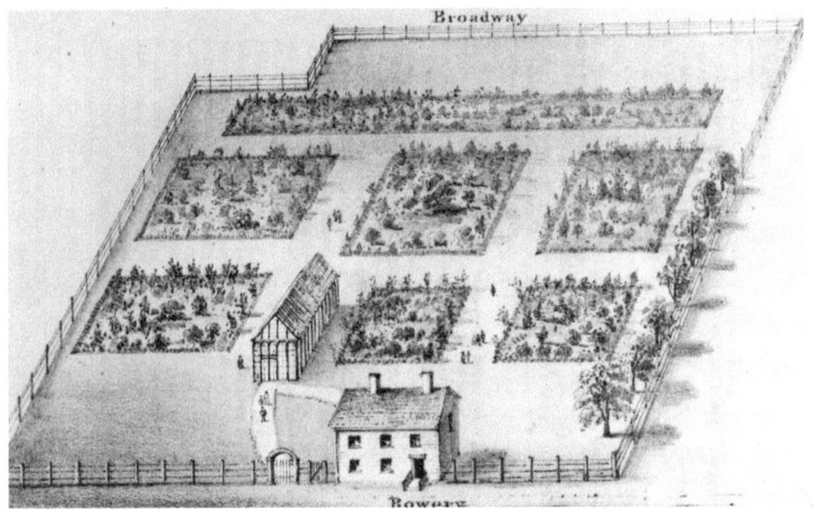

Vauxhall Garden, 1803. Library of Congress Prints and Photographs Division, Washington, DC.

In the vicinity of what is now Greenwich and Warren Streets, the Bowling Green Garden was established in the early part of the eighteenth century. It was a primitive forest, for there were no streets above Crown (now Liberty) Street on the west side, and none above Frankfort on the east. The land on which the Garden stood was a leasehold on the Church Farm. The place was given the name of the Vauxhall Garden before the middle of the same century, and for forty years thereafter was a fashionable resort and sought to be a copy of the Vauxhall in London. There was dancing and music, and groves dimly lighted where visitors could stroll, and where they might sit at tables and eat. By the time the city stretched past the locality, all that was left of the resort was what would now be called a low saloon, and its pretty garden had been sold for building lots. The second Vauxhall was off the Bowery, south of Astor Place.

A. T. Stewart's Store

Stewart Building, Broadway and Tenth Streets. NYPL Digital Collections.

The Stewart Building, on the east side of Broadway, between Chambers and Reade Streets, has undergone few external changes since it was the dry goods store of Alexander T. Stewart. On this site stood Washington Hall, which was erected in 1809. It was a hotel of the first class, and contained the fashionable ball room and banqueting-hall of the city. The building was destroyed by fire July 5, 1844. The next year Stewart, having purchased the site from the heirs of John G. Coster, began the construction of his store. Stewart came from Ireland in 1823, at the age of twenty. For a time after his arrival he was an assistant teacher in a public school. He opened a small dry goods store, and was successful. The Broadway store was opened in 1846. Four years later Stewart extended his building so that it reached Reade Street. All along Broadway by this year business houses were taking the place of residences. The Stewart residence at the northwest corner of Thirty-fourth Street and Fifth Avenue, was, at the time it was built, considered the finest house in America. Mr. Stewart died in 1876, leaving a fortune of fifty millions. His body was afterwards stolen from St. Mark's Churchyard at Tenth Street and Second Avenue.

At Broadway and Duane Street, roasted chestnuts were first sold in the street. A Frenchman stationed himself at this corner in 1828, and sold chest nuts there for so many years that he came to be reckoned as a living landmark.

At the same corner was the popular Café des Mille Colonnes, the proprietor of which, F. Palmo, afterwards built and conducted Palmo's Opera House in Chambers Street.

First Sewing Machine

In a store window on Broadway, close to Duane Street, the first sewing-machine was exhibited. A young woman sat in the window to exhibit the working of the invention to passers-by. It was regarded as an impracticable toy, and was looked at daily by many persons who considered it a curiosity unworthy of serious attention.

Masonic Hall

At Nos 314 and 316 Broadway, on the east side of the street just south of Pearl Street, stood Masonic Hall, the cornerstone of which was laid June 24, 1826. It looked imposing among the structures of the street, over which it towered, and was of the Gothic style of architecture. While it was in course of erection, William Morgan published his book which claimed to reveal the secrets of masonry. His mysterious disappearance followed, and shortly after, the rise of the anti-Masonic party and popular excitement put masonry under such a ban that the house was sold by the Order, and the name of the building was changed to Gothic Hall. On the second floor was a room looked upon as the most elegant in the United States: an imitation of the Chapel of Henry VIII, it was of Gothic architecture, furnished in richness of detail and appropriateness of design, and was one hundred feet long, fifty wide and twenty-five high. In it were held public gatherings of social and political nature.

New York Hospital

The two blocks now enclosed by Duane, Worth, Broadway and Church Streets, were occupied by the buildings and grounds of the New York Hospital. Thomas Street was afterwards cut through the grounds. As the City Hospital, the institution had been projected before the War of the Revolution. The building was completed about 1775. During the war it was used as a barrack. In 1791 it was opened for the admission of patients. On the lawn, which extended to Broadway, various societies gathered on occasions of annual parades and celebrations. The hospital buildings were in the centre of the big enclosure. At the northern end of the lawn, the present corner of Broadway and Worth Street, was the New Jerusalem Church.

Riley's Fifth Ward Hotel

On the corner of West Broadway and Franklin Street was Riley's Fifth Ward Hotel, which was a celebrated place in its day. It was the prototype of the modern elaborately fitted saloon, but was then a place of instruction and a moral resort. In a large room, reached by wide stairs from the street, were objects of interest and art in glass cases—pictures of statesmen, uniforms of the soldiers of all nations, Indian war implements, famous belongings of celebrated men, as well as such simple curiosities as a two-headed calf. On Franklin Street, before Riley's door, was a marble statue minus a head, one arm and sundry other parts. It was all that remained of the statue of the Earl of Chatham, William Pitt, which had stood in Wall Street until dragged down by British soldiers. For twenty-five years the battered wreck had lain in the corporation yard, until found and honored with a place before his door by Riley. At the latter's death the Historical Society took the remains of the statue, and it is in its rooms yet.

The passage of Washington through the island is commemorated by a tablet on a warehouse at 155 West Street, near Laight, which is inscribed:

> TO MARK THE LANDING PLACE OF
> GENERAL GEORGE WASHINGTON,
> JUNE 25, 1775,
> ON HIS WAY TO CAMBRIDGE
> TO COMMAND
> THE AMERICAN ARMY

St. John's Church

St. John's Church of Trinity Parish, in Varick Street close to Beach, was built in 1807. When the church was finished St. John's Park, occupying the entire block opposite—between Varick and Hudson, Laight and Beach Streets—was established for the exclusive use of residents whose houses faced it. Before it was established, the place had been a sandy beach that stretched to the river. The locality became the most fashionable of the city in 1825. By 1850 there had begun a gradual decline, for persons of wealth were moving uptown, and it degenerated to a tenement-house level after 1869, when the park disappeared beneath the foundations of the big freight depot which now occupies the site.

Around the corner from the church, a block away in Beach Street, is a tiny park, one of the last remnants of the Annerje Jans Farm. The bit of farm is carefully guarded now, much more so than was the entire beautiful tract. It forms a triangle and is fenced in by an iron railing, with one gate, that is fast barred and never opened. There is one struggling tree, wrapped close in winter with burlap, but it seems to feel its loneliness and does not thrive.

The Red Fort

From the centre of St. John's Park on the west, Hubert Street extends to the river. This street, now given over to manufacturers, was, in 1824, the chief promenade of the city next to the Battery Walk. It led directly to the Red Fort at the river. The fort was some distance from the shore. It was built early in the century, was round and of brick, and a bridge led to it. It was never of any practical use, but, like Castle Garden, was used as a pleasure resort.

Lispenard's Meadows

Early in the eighteenth century, Anthony Rutgers held under lease from Trinity a section of the Church Farm which took in the Dominie's Bouwerie, a property lying between where Broadway is and the Hudson River. The southern and northern lines were approximately the present Reade and Canal Streets. It was a wild spot, remaining in a primitive condition—part marsh, part swamp—covered with dwarf trees and tangled underbrush. Cattle wandered into this region and were lost. It was a dangerous place, too, for men who wandered into it. To live near it was unhealthy, because of the foul gases which abounded. It seemed to be a worthless tract. About the year 1730, Anthony Rutgers suggested to the King in Council that he would have this land drained and made wholesome and useful provided it was given to him. His argument was so strong and sensible that the land—seventy acres, now in the business section of the city—was given him and he improved it. At the northern edge of the improved waste lived Leonard Lispenard, in a farm house which was then in a northern suburb of the city, bounded by what is Hudson, Canal and Vestry Streets. Lispenard married the daughter of Rutgers, and the land falling to him it became Lispenard's Meadows.

Cows on Broadway

In Lispenard 's time Broadway ended where White Street is now and a set of bars closed the thoroughfare against cows that wandered along it. The one bit of the meadows that remains is the tiny park at the foot of Canal Street on the west side. Anthony Rutgers' homestead was close by what is Broadway and Thomas Street. After his death in 1750 it became a public house, and, with the surrounding grounds, was called Ranelagh Garden, a popular place in its time.

Lispenard Meadows. The Miriam and Ira D. Wallach Division of Art, Prints and Photographs: Print Collection, NYPL Digital Collections, https://digitalcollections.nypl.org/items/510d47da-23f0-a3d9-e040-e00a18064a99.

Canal Street

On a line with the present Canal Street, a stream ran from the Fresh Water Pond to the Hudson River, at the upper edge of Lispenard's Meadows. A project, widely and favorably considered in 1825, but which came to nothing, advocated the extension of Canal Street, as a canal, from river to river. The street took its name naturally from the little stream which was called a canal. When the street was filled in and improved, the stream was continued through a sewer leading from Centre Street. The locality at the foot of the street has received the local title of" Suicide Slip" because of the number of persons in recent years who have ended their lives by jumping into Hudson River at that point.

In Broadway, between Grand and Howard Streets, in 1819, West's circus was opened. In 1827 this was converted into a theatre called the Broadway. Later it was occupied by Tattersall's horse market.

Original Olympic Theatre

Next door to Tattersall's, at No. 444 Broadway, the original Olympic Theatre was built in 1837. W. R. Blake and Henry E. Willard built and managed the house. It was quite small and their aim had been to present plays of a high order of merit by an exceptionally good company. The latter included besides Blake, Mrs. Meander and George Barrett. After a few months of struggle against unprofitable business, prices were lowered. Little success was met with, the performances being of too artistic a nature to be popular, and Blake gave up the effort and the house. In December, 1839, Wm. Mitchell leased the house and gave performances at low prices.

At No. 453 Broadway, between Grand and Howard Streets, in 1844 John Littlefield, a corn doctor, set up a place, designating himself as a chiropodist—an occupation before unknown under that title.

At No. 485 Broadway, near Broome Street, Brougham's Lyceum was built in 1850, and opened in December with an "occasional rigmarole" and a farce. In 1852 the house was opened, September 8, as Wallack's Lyceum, having been acquired by James W. Wallack. Wallack ended his career as an actor in this house. In 1861 he removed to his new theatre, corner Thirteenth Street and Broadway. Still later the Lyceum was called the Broadway Theatre.

"Murders' Row" has its start where Watts Street ends at Sullivan, midway of the block between Grand and Broome Streets. It could not be identified by its name, for it is not a "row" at all, merely an ill-smelling alley, an arcade extending through a block of battered tenements. After running half its course through the block, the alley is broken by an intersecting space between houses—a space that is taken up by push carts, barrels, tumble-down wooden balconies; and lines of drying clothes. "Murderers' Row" is celebrated in police annals as a crime centre. But the evil doers were driven out long years ago and the houses given over to Italians. These people are excessively poor, and have such a hard struggle for life as to have no desire to regard the laws of the Health Board. Constant complaints are made that the houses are hovels and the alley a breeding-place for disease.

Greenwich Village

Greenwich Village sprang from the oldest known settlement on the Island of Manhattan. It was an Indian village, clustering about the site of the present West Washington Market, at the foot of Gansevoort Street, when Hendrick Hudson reached the island, in 1609.

The region was a fertile one, and its natural drainage afforded it sanitary advantages which even to this day make it a desirable place of residence. There was abundance of wild fowl and the waters were alive with half a hundred varieties of fish. There were sand hills, sometimes rising to a height of a hundred feet, while to the south was a marsh tenanted by wild fowl and crossed by a brook flowing from the north. It was this Minetta brook which was to mark the boundary of Greenwich Village when Governor Kieft set aside the land as a bouwerie for the Dutch West India Company. The brook arose about where Twenty-first Street now crosses Fifth Avenue, flowed to the southwest edge of Union Square, thence to Fifth Avenue and Eighth Street, across where Washington Square is, along the line of Minetta Street, and then to Hudson River, between Houston and Charlton Streets.

Sir Peter Warren

Sir Peter Warren. The Miriam and Ira D. Wallach Division of Art, Prints and Photographs: Print Collection, NYPL Digital Collections.

The interests of the little settlement were greatly advanced in 1744, when Sir Peter Warren, later the hero of Louisburg, married Susannah De Lancey and went to live there, purchasing three hundred acres of land.

Epidemics in the city from time to time drove many persons to Greenwich as a place of refuge. But it remained for the fatal yellow-fever epidemic of 1822, when 384 persons died in the city, to make Greenwich a thriving suburb instead of a struggling village. Twenty thousand persons fled the city, the greater number settling in Greenwich. Banks, public offices, stores of every sort were hurriedly opened, and whole blocks of buildings sprang up in a few days. Streets were left where lanes had been, and corn-fields were transformed into business and dwelling blocks.

Evolution of Greenwich Streets

The sudden influx of people and consequent trade into the village brought about the immediate need for street improvements. Existing streets were lengthened, footpaths and alleys were widened, but all was done without any regard to regularity. The result was the jumble of streets still to be met with in that region, where the thoroughfares are often short and often end in a cul-de-sac.

In time the streets of the City Plan crept up to those of Greenwich Village, and the village was swallowed up by the city. But it was not swallowed up so completely but that the irregular lines of the village streets are plainly to be seen on any city map.

Near where Spring Street crosses Hudson there was established, about 1765, Brannan's Garden, on the northern edge of Lispenard's Meadows. It was like the modern road-house. Greenwich Road was close to it, and pleasure seekers, who thronged the road on the way from the city to Greenwich Village, were the chief guests of the house.

Duane Street Church

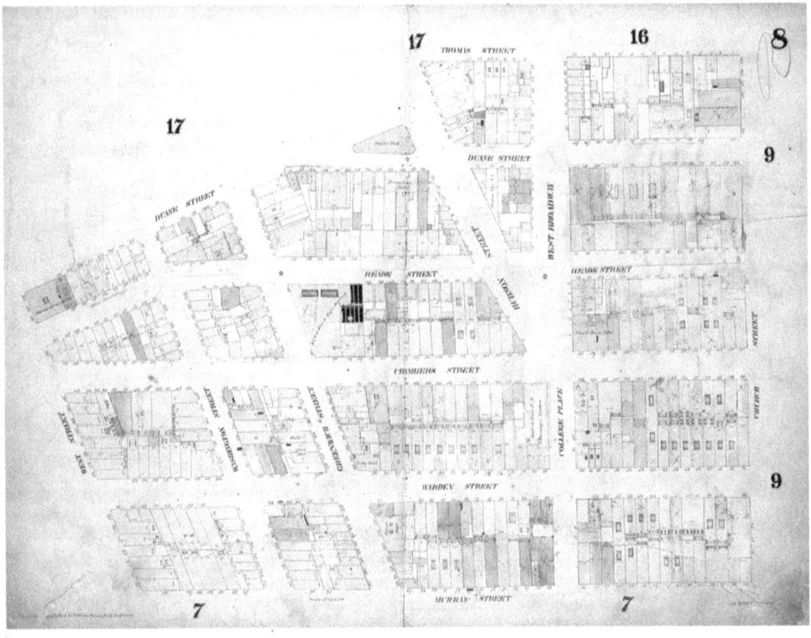

Map of Duane Street and its environs, c. 1860. Lionel Pincus and Princess Firyal Map Division, NYPL Digital Collections.

Crowded close between dwellings on the east side of Hudson Street, fifty feet south of Spring, is the Duane M. E. Church, a quaint-looking structure, half church, half business building. This is the successor of the

North Church, the North River Church and the Duane Street Church, founded in 1797, which, before it moved to Hudson Street, in 1863, was in Barley (now Duane) Street, between Hudson and Greenwich Streets.

In Spring Street, near Varick, is the Spring Street Presbyterian Church, which was built in 1825. Before its erection the "old" Spring Street Presbyterian Church stood on the site, having been built in 1811.

Richmond Hill

Although the leveling vandalism of a great city has removed every trace of Richmond Hill, the block encircled by Macdougal, Charlton, Varick and Vandam Streets, is crowded thick with memories of men and events of a past generation.

Long before there was a thought of the city getting beyond the wall that hemmed in a few scattering houses, and when the Indian settlement, which afterwards became Greenwich Village, kept close to the water's edge, a line of low sand hills called the Zandtberg, stretched their curved way from where now Eighth Street crosses Broadway, ending where Varick Street meets Vandam. At the base of the hill to the north was Manetta Creek.

The final elevation became known as Richmond Hill, and that, with a considerable tract of land, was purchased by Abraham Mortier, commissioner of the forces of George III. of England. In 1760 he built his home on the hill and called it also Richmond Hill.

Burr's Pond

The house was occupied by General Washington as his headquarters in 1776, and by Vice-President Adams in 1788. Aaron Burr obtained it in 1797, entertained lavishly there, improved the grounds, constructed an artificial lake long known as Burr's Pond, and set up a beautiful entrance gateway at what is now Macdougal and Spring Streets, which he passed through in 1804 when he went to fight his duel with Alexander Hamilton.

Burr gave up the house in 1807, and, the hill being cut away in the opening of streets in 1817, the house was lowered and rested on the north side of Charlton Street just cast of Varick. It became a theatre later and remained such until it was torn down in 1849. A quiet row of brick houses occupies the site.

St. John's Burying Ground

What is now a pleasant little park enclosed by Hudson, Leroy and Clarkson Streets, was part of a plot set aside for a graveyard when St. John's Chapel was built. It was called St. John's Burying-Ground. Its early limits extended to Carmine Street on one side and to Morton Street on the other. Under the law burials ceased there about 1850. There were 10,000 burials in the grounds, which, unlike the other Trinity graveyards, came to be neglected. The tombstones crumbled to decay, the weeds grew rank about them and the trees remained untrimmed and neglected.

About 1890 property owners in the vicinity began steps to have the burying ground made into a park. Conservative Trinity resisted the project until the city won a victory in the courts and the property was bought. Relatives of the dead were notified and some of the bodies were removed. In September, 1897, the actual work of transforming the graveyard into a park was begun. Laborers with crowbars knocked over the tombstones that still remained and putting the fragments in a pit at the eastern end of the grounds covered them with earth to make a play-spot for children.

Bedford Street Church

At Morton and Bedford Streets is the Bedford Street M. E. Church. The original structure was built in 1810 in a green pasture. Beside it was a quiet graveyard, reduced somewhat in 1830 when the church was enlarged, and wiped out when the land became valuable and the present structure was set up in 1840. The church was built for the first congregation of Methodists in Greenwich Village, formed in 1808 at the house of Samuel Walgrove at the north side of Morton Street close to Bleecker.

Where Thomas Paine Lived and Died

Thomas Paine—famous for his connection with the American and French revolutions, but chiefly for his works, "The Age of Reason," favoring Deism against Atheism and Christianity; and "Common Sense," maintaining the cause of the American colonies—died in Greenwich Village June 8, 1809, having retired there in 1802.

The final years of his life were passed in a small house in Herring (now Bleecker) Street. On the site is a double tenement numbered No. 293 Bleecker Street, southeast corner Barrow. This last named street was not opened until shortly after Paine's death. It was first called Reason Street, a compliment to the author of "The Age of Reason." This was corrupted to Raisin Street. In 1828 it was given its present name.

Shortly before his death Paine moved to a frame building set in the centre of a nearby field. Grove Street now passes over the site which is between Bleecker and West Fourth Streets, the back of the building having been where No. 59 Grove Street is now.

About the time that Barrow Street was opened Grove Street was cut through. It was called Cozine Street, then Columbia, then Burrows, and finally, in 1829, was changed to Grove. When the street was widened in 1836, the house in which Paine had died, until then left standing, was demolished.

Admiral Warren and His Family

The homestead of Admiral Sir Peter Warren occupied the ground now taken up in the solidly built block bounded by Charles, Fourth, Bleecker and Perry Streets. The house was built in 1744, in the midst of green fields, and for more than a century it was the most important dwelling in Greenwich. Admiral Warren of the British Navy was, next to the Governor, the most important person in the Province. His house was the favorite resort of social and influential New York. The Admiral's influence and popularity had a marked effect on the village, which, by his coming, was given an impetus that made it a thriving place.

Of the three daughters of Admiral Warren, Charlotte, the eldest, married Willoughby, Earl of Abingdon; the second, Ann, married Charles Fitzroy, afterwards Baron Southampton, and Susannah, the youngest, married William Skinner, a Colonel of Foot. These marriages had their effect also on Greenwich Village, serving to continue the prosperity of the place. Roads which led through the district, of which the Warren family controlled a great part, were named in honor of the different family branches. The only name now surviving is that of Abingdon Square.

In the later years of his life, Sir Peter Warren represented the City of Westminster in Parliament. He was buried in Westminster Abbey.

State Prison

In 1796 the State Prison was built on about four acres of ground, surrounded by high walls, and taking in the territory now enclosed by Washington,

West, Christopher and Perry Streets. The site is now, for the most part, occupied by a brewery, but traces of the prison walls are yet to be seen in those of the brewery. There was a wharf at the foot of Christopher Street. In 1826 the prison was purchased by the Corporation of the State. The construction of a new State Prison had begun at Sing Sing in 1825. In 1828 the male prisoners were transferred to Sing Sing, and the female prisoners the next year.

Convict Labor

The yard of the early prison extended down to the river, there were fields about and a wide stretch of beach. It was here that the first system of prison manufactures was organized. A convict named Noah Gardner, who was a shoemaker, induced the prison officials to permit him the use of his tools. In a short time he had trained most of the convicts into a skilled body of shoemakers.

The gathering together of a number of convicts in a workroom was at first productive of some disorder, owing to the difficulty of keeping them under proper discipline under the new conditions. In 1799 came the first riot. The keepers fired upon and killed several convicts. There was another revolt in 1803.

Gardner had been found guilty of forgery, but was reprieved on the gallows through the influence of the Society of Friends, of which he was a member, and sentenced to life imprisonment. Because of his services in organizing the prison work, he was liberated after serving seven years. Becoming then a shoe manufacturer, he was successful for several years, when he absconded, taking with him a pretty Quakeress, and was never heard of again.

Quaint Houses in Wiehawken Street

Although the prison has been swept away, an idea of its locality can he had from the low buildings at the west side of nearby Wiehawken Street. These buildings have stood for more than a hundred years, having been erected before the prison.

Old Houses ·Wiebawken St·

That part of Greenwich Village that was transformed from fields into a town in a few days, during the yellow fever scare of 1822, centered at the point where West Eleventh Street crosses West Fourth Street. At this juncture was a cornfield on which, in two days, a hotel capable of accommodating three hundred guests was built. At the same time a hundred other houses sprang up, as if by magic, on all sides.

Bank Street

Bank Street was named in 1799. The year previous a clerk in the Bank of New York on Wall Street was one of the earliest victims of yellow fever, and the officials decided to take precautions in case of the bank being quarantined at a future time. Eight lots were purchased on a then nameless lane in Greenwich Village. The bank was erected there, and gave the lane the name of Bank Street.

Washington Square

Washington Square was once a Potter's Field. A meadow was purchased by the city for this purpose in 1789, and the pauper graveyard was established about where the Washington Arch is now.

Manetta Creek, coming from the north, flowed to the west of the arch site, crossed to what is now the western portion of the Square, ran through the present Minetta Street and on to the river. In 1795, during a yellow fever epidemic, the field was used as a common graveyard. In 1797 the pauper graveyard which had been in the present Madison Square, was abandoned in favor of this one. There was a gallows on the ground and criminals were executed and interred on the spot as late as 1822.

Looking South from Minetta Lane

In 1823 the Potter's Field was abandoned and removed to the present Bryant Park at Forty-second Street and Sixth Avenue. In 1827, three and one half acres of ground were added to the plot and the present Washington Square was opened.

Obelisk Lane

Past the pauper graveyard ran an inland road to Greenwich Village. This extended from the Post Road (now the Bowery) at the present Astor Place near Cooper Union, continued in a direct line to about the position of the Washington Arch, and from that point to the present Eighth Avenue just above Fifteenth Street. This road, established through the fields in 1768, was called Greenwich Lane. It was also known as Monument Lane and Obelisk Lane. A small section of it still exists in Astor Place from Bowery to Broadway. A larger section is Greenwich Avenue from Eighth to Fourteenth Streets. Monument Lane took its name from a monument at Fifteenth Street where the road ended, which had been erected to the memory of General Wolfe, the hero of Quebec. The monument disappeared in a mysterious way during the British occupation. It is thought to have been destroyed by soldiers.

Graveyard In a Side Street

A few feet east of Sixth Avenue, on the south side of Eleventh Street, is a brick wall and railing, behind which can be seen several battered tombstones in a triangular plot of ground. This is all that is left of a Jewish graveyard established almost a century ago.

Milligan's Lane was the continuation of Amos (now West Tenth) Street, from Greenwich Avenue to Twelfth Street where it joined the Union Road. This lane struck the line of Sixth A venue where Eleventh Street is now. At the southwest corner of this junction the course of the lane can be seen yet in the peculiar angle of the side wall of a building there, and in a similar angle of other houses near by. Close by this corner the second graveyard of Shearith Israel Synagogue was established early in this century. It took the place of the Beth Haim, or Place of Rest, down town, a remnant of which is to be seen in New Bowery off Chatham Square.

Milligan's Lane

The Eleventh Street graveyard, established in the midst of green fields, fronted on Milligan's Lane and extended back 110 feet. When Eleventh Street was cut through under the conditions of the City Plan, in 1830, it passed directly through the graveyard, cutting it away so that only the tiny portion now there was left. At that time a new place of burial was opened in Twenty-first Street west of Sixth Avenue.

Union Road

At a point just behind the house numbered 33 Eleventh Street, midway of the block between Fifth and Sixth Avenues, Union Road had its starting point. It was a short road, forming a direct communicating line between Skinner and Southampton Roads. Skinner Road, running from Hudson River along the line of the present Christopher Street, ended where Union Road met Southampton. Skinner Road, running from Hudson River along the line of the present Christopher Street, ended where Union Road began; and Union Road met Southampton at what is now the corner of Fifteenth Street and Seventh Avenue. This point was also the junction of Southampton and Great Kiln Roads.

Evidences of the Union Road are still to be seen in Twelfth Street, at the projecting angle of the houses numbered 43 and 45· It was just at this point that Milligin's Lane ended. On Thirteenth Street, the course of Union Road is shown by the slanting wall of a big business building, numbered 36.

First Presbyterian Church

In Twelfth Street, between Sixth and Seventh Avenues, is the First Reformed Presbyterian Church. The congregation was started as a praying society in 1790 at the house of John Agnew at No. 9 Peck Slip. In 1798 the congregation worshipped in a school house in Cedar Street. They soon after built their first church at Nos. 39 and 41 Chambers Street, where the American News Company building is now. It was a frame building, and was succeeded in 1818 by a brick .building on the same site. In 1834 a new church was erected at Prince and Marion Streets. The foundation for the present church was laid in 1848, and the church occupied it in the following year.

Society Library

The New York Society Library. The Miriam and Ira D. Wallach Division of Art, Prints and Photographs: Print Collection, NYPL Digital Collections.

The New York Society Library, at 107 University Place, near Fourteenth Street, claims to be the oldest institution of its kind in America. It is certainly the most interesting in historical associations, richness of old literature and art works. It is the direct outcome of the library established in 1700, with quarters in the City Hall, in Wall Street, by Richard, Earl of Bellmont, the Governor of New York.

In 1754 an association was incorporated for carrying on a library, and their collection, added to the library already in existence, was called the City Library. The Board of Trustees consisted of the most prominent men in the city. In 1772 a charter was granted by George III, under the name of the New York Society Library.

During the Revolutionary War the books became spoil for British soldiers. Many were destroyed and many sold. After the war the remains of the library were gathered from various parts of the city and again collected in the City Hall. In 1784 the members of the Federal Congress deliberated in the library rooms. In 1795 the library was moved to Nassau Street, opposite the Middle Dutch Church; in 1836 to Chambers Street; in 1841 to Broadway and Leonard Street; in 1853 to the Bible House, and in 1856 to the present building.

Great Kiln Road

At the point that is now Seventh Avenue and Fifteenth Street, then intersected by the Union Road, the Great Kiln Road ended. Its continuation was called Southampton Road. From that point it continued to Nineteenth Street, east of Sixth Avenue, and then parallel with Sixth Avenue to Love Lane, the present Twenty-first Street.

The line of this road, where it joined the Great Kiln Road, is still clearly shown in the oblique side wall of the house at the northwest corner of Seventh Avenue and Fifteenth Street. Here, also, it has a marked effect on t:he east wall of St. Joseph's Home for the Aged. The first-mentioned house, with the cutting through of the streets, has been left one of those queer triangular buildings, with full front and running to a point in the rear.

Weavers' Row

When the road reached what is now Sixteenth Street, a third of a block east of Seventh Avenue, it passed through the block in a sweeping curve to the present corner of Seventeenth Street and Sixth Avenue. The evidence of its passage is still to be seen in the tiny wooden houses buried in the centre of the block, which are remnants of a row called Paisley Place, or Weavers' Row. This row was built during the yellow-fever agitation of 1822, and was occupied by Scotch weavers who operated their hand machines there.

The road took its name from Sir Peter Warren's second daughter, who married Charles Fitzroy, who later became the Baron Southampton.

Graveyard Behind a Store

In Twenty-first Street, a little west of Sixth Avenue, is the unused though not uncared-for graveyard of the Shearith Israel Synagogue. The graveyard cannot be seen from the street, but from the rear windows of a near-by dry-goods store a glimpse can be had of the ivy-covered receiving-vault and the time-grayed tombstones.

When this "Place of Rest" was established the locality was all green fields. The graveyard had been forced from further down town by the cutting through of Eleventh Street in 1830. Interments were made in this spot until 1852, when the cemetery was removed to Cypress Hills, L. I., the Common Council having in that year prohibited burials within the city limits. But though there were no burials, the congregation have persistently refused to sell this plot, just as they have the earlier plots, the remains of which are off Chatham Square and in Eleventh Street, near Sixth Avenue.

Love Lane

Abingdon Road in the latter years of its existence was commonly called Love Lane, and more than a century ago followed close on the line of the present Twenty-first Street from what is now Broadway to Eighth Avenue. It was the northern limit of a tract of land given by the city to Admiral Sir Peter Warren in recognition of his services at the capture of Louisburg.

From this road, when the Warren estate was divided among the daughters of the Admiral, two roads, the Southampton and the Warren, were opened through this upper part of the estate.

The name Love Lane was given to the road in the latter part of the eighteenth century, and was retained until it was swallowed up in Twenty-first Street. This last was ordered opened in 1827, but was not actually opened until some years later. There is no record to show where the name came from. The generally accepted idea is that being a quiet and little traveled spot, it was looked upon as a lane where happy couples might drive, far from the city, and amid green fields and stately trees confide the story of their loves. It was the longest drive from the town, by way of the Post Road, Bloomingdale Road and so across the west to Southampton, Great Kiln roads, through Greenwich Village and by the river road back to town.

The road originally took its name from the oldest daughter of Admiral Warren, who married the Earl of Abingdon.

There are still traces of Love Lane in Twenty-first Street. The two houses numbered 25 and 27 stood on the road. The houses 51, 53 and 55, small and odd appearing, are more closely identified with the lane. When built, these houses were conspicuous and alone, at the junction where Southampton Road from Greenwich Village ran into Love Lane. They are thought to have been a single house serving as a tavern.

Close by, at the northeast corner of Twenty-first Street and Sixth Avenue, the house with the gable roof is one that also stood on the old road, though built at a later date than the three next to it.

The road ended for many years about on the line with the present Eighth Avenue, where it ran into the Fitzroy Road. Some years previous to the laying out of the streets under the City Plan in 1811, Love Lane was continued to Hudson River. Before it reached the river it was crossed, a little east of Seventh Avenue, by the Warren Road, although there is no trace of the crossing now.

Chelsea Village

Although Chelsea Village was long ago swallowed up by the city, and its boundaries blotted out by the rectangular lines of that plan under which the streets were mapped out in 1811, there is still a suggestion of it in the green lawns and gray buildings of the General Theological Seminary of the Protestant Episcopal Church, which occupies the block between Twentieth and Twenty-first Streets, Ninth and Tenth Avenues. Chelsea got its name in 1750, when Captain Thomas Clarke, an old soldier, gave the name to his country seat, in remembrance of the English home for invalided soldiers. It was between two and three miles from the city, a stretch of country land along the Hudson River with not another house anywhere near it. The house stood, as streets are now, at the south side of Twenty-third Street, about two hundred feet west of Ninth Avenue, on a hill that sloped to the river. The captain had hoped to die in his retreat, but his home was burned to the ground during his severe illness, and he died in the home of his nearest neighbor. Soon after his death the house was rebuilt by his widow, Mrs. Mollie Clarke. The latter dying in 1802, a portion of the estate with the house went to Bishop Benjamin Moore, who had married Mrs. Clarke's daughter, Charity. It passed from him in 1813 to his son, Clement C. Moore. The latter reconstructed the house, and it stood until 1850.

Clement C. Moore 's estate was included within the present lines of Eighth Avenue, Nineteenth to Twenty-fourth Streets and Hudson River. These are approximately the bounds of Chelsea Village which grew up around the old Chelsea homestead. It came to be a thriving village, conveniently reached by the road to Greenwich and then by Fitzroy Road; or by the Bowery Road, Bloomingdale, and then along Love Lane.

London Terrace

In 1831 the streets were cut through and the village thereafter grew up on the projected lines of the City Plan. It was for this reason that Chelsea, when the city reached it, was merged into it so perfectly that there is not an imperfect street line to tell where the village had been and where the city joined it. There are houses of the old village still standing; notably those still called the Chelsea Cottages in Twenty-fourth Street west of Ninth Avenue, and the row called the London Terrace in Twenty-third Street between Ninth and Tenth Avenues.

The block on which the General Theological Seminary stands was given to the institution by Clement C. Moore, and was long called Chelsea Square. The cornerstone of the East Building was laid in 1825, and of the West Building, which still stands, in 1835.

It was this Clement C. Moore, living quietly in the village that had grown up around him, who wrote the child's poem which will be remembered longer than its writer—"'Twas the Night before Christmas."

III

Oliver Street Baptist Church

The Oliver Street Baptist Church was built on the northwest corner of Oliver and Henry Streets in 1795. It was rebuilt in 1800, and again in 1819. Later it was burned, and finally restored in 1843. The structure is now occupied by the Mariners' Temple, and the record of its burning is to be seen on a marble tablet on the front wall.

Oliver Street—that is, the two blocks from Chatham Square to Madison Street—was called Fayette Street before the name was changed to Oliver in 1825.

James Street was once St. James Street. The change was made prior to 1816.

Mariners' Church, at 46 Catherine Street, was erected in 1854, on the southeast corner of Madison Street. Prior to that, and as far back as 1819, it had been at 76 Roosevelt Street.

Madison Street

Banker Street having become a byword, because of the objectionable character of its inhabitants, the name was changed to Madison Street in 1826.

Between Jefferson and Clinton Streets, and south of Henry, was a pond, the only bit of water which, in early days, emptied into the East River between what afterward became Roosevelt Street and Houston Street. A wet meadow, rather than a distinct stream, extended from this pond to the river as an outlet. This became later the region of shipyards.

Where Nathan Hale Was Hanged

On what is now Cherry Street, between Clinton and Jefferson Streets, was the house of Col. Henry Rutgers, the Revolutionary patriot, and his farm extended from that point in all directions. On a tree of this farm Nathan Hale, the martyr spy of the Revolution, was hanged, September 22, 1776. On this same farm the Church of the Sea and Land, still standing with its three-foot walls, at Market and Henry Streets, was built in 1817.

· Church of Sea & Land ·

In 1828, at the corner of Henry and Scammel Streets, was erected All Saints' Church (Episcopal). It still stands, now hemmed in by dwelling-houses. It is a low rock structure. A bit of green, a stunted tree and some shrubs still struggle through the bricks at the rear of the church, and can be seen through a tall iron railing from narrow Scammel Street. In 1825 the church occupied a chapel on Grand Street at the comer of Columbia.

First Tenement House

The first house designed especially for many tenants was built in 1833, in Water Street just east of Jackson, on which site is now included Corlears Hook Park. It was four stories in height, and arranged for one family on each floor. It was built by Thomas Price, and owned by James P. Allaire, whose noted engine works were close by in Cherry Street, between Walnut (now Jackson) and Corlears Street.

Where Grand and Pitt Streets cross is the top of a hill formerly known as Mount Pitt. On this hill the building occupied by the Mount Pitt Circus was built in 1826. It was burned in 1828.

At Grand, corner of Ridge Street, is the St. Mary's Church (Catholic), which was built in 1833, a rough stone structure with brick front and back. In 1826 it was in Sheriff between Broome and Delancey Streets. It had the first Roman Catholic bell in the city. In 1831 the church was burned by a burglar, and the new structure was built in Grand Street.

Actual work on the pier for the new East River Bridge, at the foot of Delancey Street, was begun in the spring of 1897.

Manhattan Island

Much confusion has arisen, and still exists, in the designation of the territory under the names of Manhattan Island and Island of Manhattan. The two islands a hundred years ago were widely different bodies. They are joined now. Manhattan Island was the name given to a little knoll of land which land within the limits of what is now Third, Houston and Lewis Streets and the East River. At high tide the place was a veritable island. There seems to be still a suggestion of it in the low buildings which occupy the ground of the former island. About the ancient boundary, as though closing it in, are tall tenements and factory buildings. On the grounds of this old island the first recreation pier was built, in 1897, at the foot of Third Street.

The Island of Manhattan has always been the name applied to the land occupied by the old City of New York, now the Borough of Manhattan.

In the heart of the block surrounded by Rivington, Stanton, Goerck and Mangin Streets, there is still to be seen the remains of a slanting-roofed market, closed in by the houses which have been built about it. It was set up in 1827, and named Manhattan Market after the nearby island.

Bone Alley

· Bone Alley ·

Work on the Hamilton Fish Park was begun in 1896, in the space bounded by Stanton, Houston, Pitt and Sheriff Streets, then divided into two blocks by Willett Street. This was a congested, tenement-house vicinity, where misery and poverty pervaded most of the dingy dwellings. In wiping out the two solidly built-up blocks, Bone Alley, well known in police history for a generation, was effaced. On the west side of Willett Street, midway of the block, Bone Alley had its start and extended sixty feet into the block—a twenty-five foot space between tall tenements, running plump into a row of houses extending horizontal with it. When these houses were erected they each had long gardens, which were built upon when the land became too valuable to be spared for flower-beds or breathing-spots. In time they became the homes of rag- and bone-pickers, and thus the alley which led to them got its name, which it kept even after the rag-pickers and the law-breakers who succeeded them had been driven away by the police.

There was, forty years ago, a well of good, drinkable water at the point where Rivington and Columbia Streets now cross.

"Mother" Mandelbaum

The little frame house at the northwest corner of Rivington and Clinton Streets was the home of "Mother" Frederica Mandelbaum for many years, until she was driven from the city in 1884. This "Queen of the Crooks," receiver of stolen goods and friend of all the criminal class, compelled, in a sense, the admiration of the police, who for years battled in vain to outwit her cleverness. When the play, "The Two Orphans," was first produced, Mrs. Wilkins, as the "Frochard," copied the character of "Mother" Mandelbaum and gave a representation of the woman that all who knew the original recognized. Other plays were written, and also many stories, having her as a central figure. She died at Hamilton, Ontario, in 1894.

At the crossing of Rivington and Suffolk Streets was the source of Stuyvesant's Creek. Frum there, as the streets exist now, it crossed Stanton Street, near Clinton; Houston, at Sheriff; Second, near Houston; then wound around to the north of Manhattan Island, and emptied into the East River at Third Street.

Allen Street Memorial Church

In Rivington Street, between Ludlow and Orchard, is the Allen Street Memorial Church (M. E.), built in 1888. The original Church, which was built in 1810, is two blocks away, in Allen Street, between Delancey and Rivington Streets. It was rebuilt in 1836, and when the new Rivington Street structure was erected the old house was sold to a Jewish congregation, who still occupy it as a synagogue.

In Grand Street, between Essex and Ludlow Streets, the Essex Market was built in 1818. The court next to it, in Essex Street, was built in 1856.

Mile Stone On the Bowery

On the Bowery, opposite Rivington Street, is a milestone (one of three that yet remain) which formerly marked the distance from the City Hall, in Wall Street, on the Post Road. The land to the east of the Bowery belonged to James De Lancey, who was Chief Justice of the Colony in 1733,and in 1753 became Lieutenant-Governor. A lane led from the Bowery, close by the milestone, to his country house, which was at the present northwest corner of Delancey and Christie Streets. It was in this house that he died suddenly in 1760. James De Lancey was the eldest son of Etienne (Stephen) De Lancey, who built the house which afterwards was known as Fraunces' Ta\'ern, and which still stands at Broad and Pearl Streets. He later built the homestead at Broadway and Cedar Street. Originally the name was "de Lanci." It became "de Lancy" in the seventeenth century, and was Anglicized in the eighteenth century to "De Lancey."

Where Grand Street crosses Mulberry was, until 1802, the family burial vault of the Bayard family, it having been the custom of early· settlers to bury their dead near their homesteads. The locality was called Bunker Hill.

St. Patrick's Church

St. Patrick's Church, enclosed now by the high wall at Mott and Prince Streets, was completed in 1815, the cornerstone having been laid in 1809. It was surrounded by meadows and great primitive trees. This region was so wild that in 1820 a fox was killed in the churchyard. In 1866 the interior of the church was destroyed by fire. It was at once reconstructed in its present form. Amongst others buried in the vaults are "Boss" John Kelly, Vicar-General Starr and Bishop Connelly, first resident bishop of New York.

At Prince and Marion Streets, northwest corner, the house in which President James Monroe lived while in the city still stands.

An Unsolved Crime

St. Nicholas Hotel. The Miriam and Ira D. Wallach Division of Art, Prints and Photographs: Print Collection, NYPL Digital Collections.

The St. Nicholas Hotel was at Broadway and Spring Street, and on the ground floor John Anderson kept a tobacco store, to which the attention of the entire country was directed in July, 1842, because of the murder of Mary Rogers. This tragedy gave Edgar Allan Poe material for his story "The Mystery of Marie Roget," into which he introduced every detail of the actual happening. Mary Rogers was a saleswoman in the tobacco store, and being young and pretty she attracted considerable attention. She disappeared one July day, and, soon after, her body was found drowned near the Sibyl's Cave at Hoboken. The deepest mystery surrounded her evident murder, and much interest was taken in attempts at a solution, but it remained an unsolved crime.

Niblo's Garden

On the cast side of Broadway, between Prince and Houston Streets, on July 4, 1828, William Niblo opened his Garden, Hotel and Theatre, to be known for many years thereafter as Niblo's Garden. Prior to that, he had kept the Bank Coffee House, at William and Pine Streets.

The Metropolitan Hotel was built in Niblo's Garden, on the corner that is now Broadway and Prince Street, in 1852, at a cost of a million dollars. The theatre in the hotel building was called Niblo's Garden. The building was demolished in 1894, and a business block was put up on the site.

Across the street from Niblo's, on Broadway, in a modest brick house, lived, at one time, James Fenimore Cooper, the novelist.

At No. 624 Broadway, between Houston and Bleecker Streets, was Laura Keene's theatre. On March 1, 1858, Polly Marshall made her first appearance on any stage at that theatre. Later it became the Olympic Theatre.

At Broadway and Bleecker Streets, a well was drilled, in 1832, which was four hundred and forty-eight feet deep, and which yielded forty-four thousand gallons of water a day.

Tripler Hall

Tripler Hall was at No. 677 Broadway, near Bond Street. Adelina Patti appeared there on September 22, 1852, when ten years old, giving evidence of her future greatness. She sang there for some time, usually accompanied by the boy violinist, Paul Julien.

Tripler Hall had been renamed the Metropolitan Hall, when it was destroyed by fire in 1854. Lafarge House, which stood next it, was also burned. The house was rebuilt on the site, and opened in September, 1854, under the name of the New York Theatre and Metropolitan Opera House.

Rachel the great was first seen in America at this house, September 3, 1855. Later the house became the Winter Garden.

First Marble-Fronted Houses

The first marble-fronted houses in the city were built on Broadway, opposite Bond Street, in 1825. They were called the Marble Houses, and attracted much attention. Being far out of the city, excursions were made to view them. Afterwards they became the Tremont House, and are still in use as a hotel.

A pipe for a well was sunk in Broadway, opposite Bond Street, in April, 1827, it being thought that enough water for the supply of the immediate neighborhood could be obtained therefrom. The water was not found, however.

Burdell Murder

Harvey Burdell. The Miriam and Ira D. Wallach Division of Art, Prints and Photographs: Print Collection, New York Public Library.

No. 31 Bond Street was the scene of a celebrated murder. The house is torn down now, but it was identical with the one which now stands at No. 29. On January 3, 1857, Dr. Harvey Burdell, a dentist, was literally butchered there, being stabbed fifteen times. A portion of the house had been occupied by a widow named Cunningham, and her two daughters. After the murder, Mrs. Cunningham claimed a widow's share of the Doctor's estate, on the ground that she had been married to him some months before.

This claim started an investigation, which resulted in Mrs. Cunningham's being suspected of the crime, arrested, tried and acquitted. Soon after her acquittal, she attempted to secure control of the entire Burdell estate, by claiming that she had given birth to an heir to the property. The scheme failed, for the physician through whom she obtained a new-born child from Bellevue Hospital, disclosed the plot to District Attorney A. Oakey Hall. The woman and her daughters left the city suddenly, and were not heard of again. The mystery of the murder was never solved.

The part of Houston Street east of the Bowery was, prior to November, 1833, called North Street. At the time the change in names was made the street was raised. Between Broadway and the Bowery had been a wet tract of land many feet below the grade. In 1844 the street was extended from Lewis Street to the East River.

The Bleecker Street Bank, which was just east of Broadway, on the north side of Bleecker Street, was moved in October, 1897, to Twenty-first Street and Fourth Avenue, and called The Bank for Savings. It had originally been in the New York Institute Building in City Hall Park.

Marble Cemetery

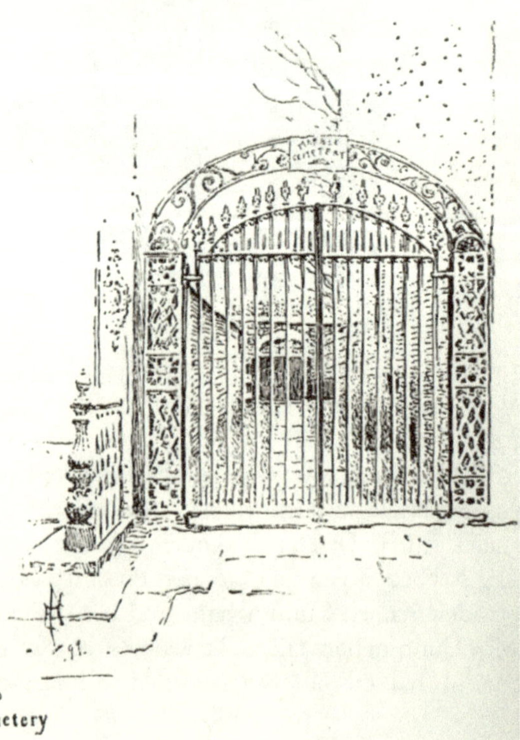

Entrance to
Marble Cemetery

In the heart of the block enclosed by the Bowery, Second Avenue, Second and Third Streets, is a hidden grave- yard. It is the New York Marble Cemetery, and so completely has it been forgotten that its name no longer appears in the City Directory. On four sides it is hemmed about by tenements and business buildings, so that one could walk past it for a lifetime without knowing that it was there. On the Second Avenue side, the entrance is formed by a narrow passage between houses, which is closed by an iron gateway. But the gate is always locked, and at the opposite end of the passage is another gate of wood set in a brick wall, so high that nothing but the tops of trees can be seen beyond it. From the upper rear windows of the neighboring tenements a view of the place can be had. It is a wild spot, four hundred feet by one hundred, covered by a tangled growth of bushes and weeds, crossed by neglected paths, and enclosed by a wall seventeen feet high There is no sign of a tombstone. In the southwest corner is a deadhouse of roughhewn stone. On the south wall the names of vault owners are chiseled. Among these were some of the best known New Yorkers fifty years ago. The records of the city show that this land was owned by Henry Eckford and Marion, his wife. They deeded it to Anthony Dey and George W. Strong when the cemetery corporation was organized, July 30, 1830. There were one hundred and fifty-six vaults, and fifteen hundred persons were buried there. This cemetery is forgotten almost as completely as its own dead, and its memories do not molest the dwellers in the surrounding tenements who overlook it from their rear windows, and use it as a sort of dumping-ground for all useless things that can readily be thrown into it.

The Second Marble Cemetery

There is another Marble Cemetery which historians sometimes confuse with this hidden graveyard, namely, one on Second Street, between First and Second Avenues. Some of the larger merchants of the city bought the ground in 1831, and created the New York City Marble Cemetery. Among the original owners was Robert Lenox. When he died, in 1839, his body was placed in a vault of the First Presbyterian Church at 16 Wall Street. When that church was removed to Fifth Avenue and Twelfth Street the remains of Lenox with others were removed to this Marble Cemetery. The body of President James Monroe was first interred here, but was removed in 1859 to Virginia. Thomas Addis Emmet, the famous jurist, is also buried here. One of the most conspicuous monuments in St. Paul's churchyard, the shaft at the right of the church, was erected to the memory of Emmet.

A large column on the other side of the church preserves the memory of another man whose body does not lie in the churchyard, for William James Macneven was interred in the burying-ground of the Riker family at Bowery Bay, L.I.

In Second Street, between Avenue A and First Avenue, stood a Methodist church, and beside it a graveyard, until 1840; when the building was turned into a public school. There were fifteen hundred bodies in the yard, but they were not removed to Evergreen Cemetery until 1860. Only fifteen bodies were claimed by relatives. One man who applied for his father's body refused that offered him, claiming that the skull was too small, and that some mistake had been made in disinterment.

Second Street Methodist Episcopal Church, between Avenues C and D, was built in 1832, the congregation having previously worshipped in private houses in the vicinity. At one time this was the most prominent and wealthiest church on the eastern side of the city.

Bouwerie Village

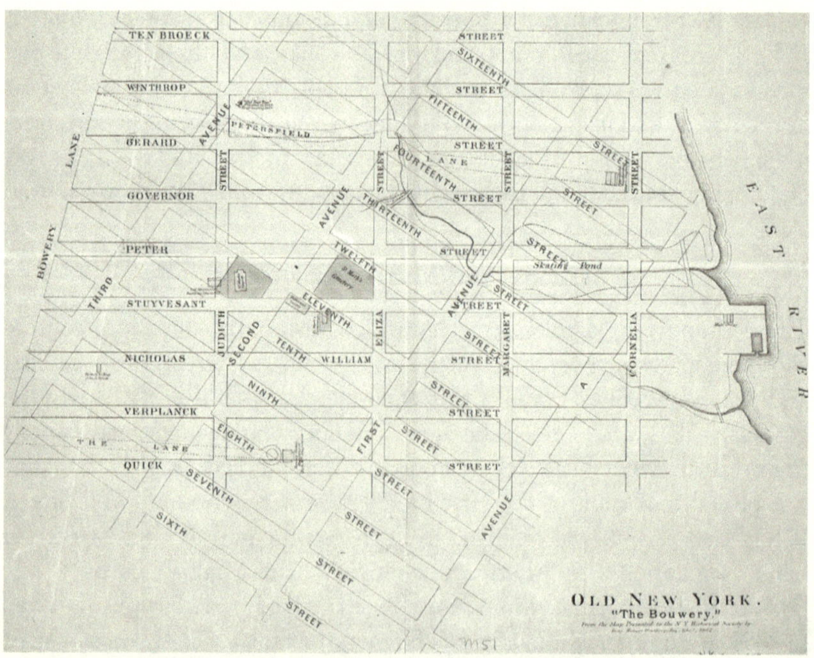

Bouwerie Village Map. Lionel Pincus and Princess Firyal Map Division, New York Public Library, NYPL Digital Collections.

The Bouwerie Village was another of the little settlements—once a busy spot, but now so effaced that every outline of its existence is blotted out. It centered about the site of the present St. Mark's Church, Second Avenue and Tenth Street. In 1651, when Peter Stuyvesant, the last of the Dutch Governors, had ruled four years, he purchased the Great Bouwerie, a tract of land extending two miles along the river north of what is now Grand Street, taking in a section of the present Bowery and Third Avenue. As there was, from time to time, trouble with the Indians, the Governor ordered the dwellers on his bouwerie, as well as those on adjoining bouweries, to form a village and gather there for mutual protection at the first sign of an outbreak. Very soon the settlement included a blacksmith's shop, a tavern and a dozen houses. In this way the Bouwerie Village was started. Peter Stuyvesant in time built a chapel, and in it Hermanus Van Hoboken, the schoolmaster, after whom the city of Hoboken is named, preached. Years after the founding of the village, when New Amsterdam had become New York, and when the old Governor had returned from Holland, where he had, before the States-General, fought for vindication in so readily giving up the province to the English, Stuyvesant returned to end his days in the Bouwerie Village. He died there at the age of eighty, and was buried in the graveyard of the Bouwerie Church. St. Mark's Church, at Tenth Street and Second Avenue, stands on the site of the old church, and a memorial stone to Peter Stuyvesant is still to be seen under the porch. It reads :

IN THIS VAULT LIES BURIED
PETRUS STUYVESANT,
LATE CAPTAIN-GENERAL AND GOVERNOR IN CHIEF
OF AMSTERDAM IN NEW NETHERLAND
NOW CALLED NEW YORK
AND THE DUTCH WEST INDIES, DIED IN A.D. 167 1/2
AGED 80 YEARS.

Grave of Peter Stuyvesant

When Judith, the widow of Peter Stuyvesant, died, in 1692, she left the church in which the old Governor had worshipped to the Dutch Reformed Church. A condition was that the Stuyvesant vault should be forever protected. By 1793 the church had fallen into decay. Then another Peter Stuyvesant, great-grandson of the Dutch Governor, who was a vestryman of Trinity Church, gave the site and surrounding lots, together with $2,000, and the Trinity Corporation added $12,500, and erected the present St. Mark's Church. The cornerstone was laid in 1795 and the building completed in 1799. It had no steeple until 1829, when that portion was added. In 1858 the porch was added. In the churchyard were buried the remains of Mayor Philip Hone and of Governor Daniel D. Tompkins. It was here that the body of Alexander T. Stewart rested until stolen. Close by the church was the mansion of Governor Stuyvesant. It was an imposing structure for those days, built of tiny bricks brought from Holland. A fire destroyed the house at the time of the Revolution.

When Peter Stuyvesant returned from Holland he brought with him a pear tree, which he planted in a garden near his Bouwerie Village house. This tree flourished for more than two hundred years. At Thirteenth Street and Third Avenue, on the house at the northeast corner, is a tablet inscribed:

ON THIS CORNER GREW
PETRUS STUYVESANT'S PEAR TREE

RECALLED TO HOLLAND IN 1664,
ON HIS RETURN
HE BROUGHT THE PEAR TREE
AND PLANTED IT
AS HIS MEMORIAL,
"BY WHICH," SAID HE, "MY NAME
MAY BE REMEMBERED."
THE PEAR TREE FLOURISHED
AND BORE FRUIT FOR OVER
TWO HUNDRED YEARS

THIS TABLET IS PLACED HERE BY
THE HOLLAND SOCIETY
OF NEW YORK
SEPTEMBER, 1890.

First Sunday School

In 1785 half a dozen persons in the Bouwerie Village, then scattering to the east from the site of Cooper Union, met at the "Two Mile Stone"—so called from being two miles from Federal Hall—in the upper room of John Coutant's house, on the site where Cooper Institute stands now. The room was used as a shoe store during the week. Here, on Sundays, ministers from the John Street Church instructed converts. Peter Cooper, who was a member of the church, a few years later conceived the idea of connecting the school with the church. The organization was perfected, and he was chosen Superintendent of this, the first Sunday School of New York.

The quarters becoming cramped, in 1795 the congregation moved to a two-story building a block away, on Nicholas William Street. This street, long since blotted out, extended from what is now Fourth Avenue and Seventh Street, across the Cooper Institute site and part of the adjoining block, to Eighth (now St. Mark's Place), midway of the block between Third and Second Avenues. The street was named after Nicholas William Stuyvesant.

Bowery Village Church

When the old John Street Church was taken down, in 1817, the timber from it was used to erect a church next to the Sunday School (called the Academy). This church was called the Bowery Village Church. In 1830, the Bowery Village Church having been wiped out by the advancing streets of the City Plan, Nicholas William Street went with it, and a church was then established a short distance to the east, on the line of what is now Seventh Street, north side, and this became the Seventh Street Church. In 1837 persons living near by who objected to the church revivals presented the trustees with two lots, nearer Third Avenue. There a new church was built, which still stands.

Second Vauxhall Garden

Vauxhall Garden occupied (according to the present designation of the streets) the space south of Astor Place, between Fourth Avenue and

Broadway, to the line of Fifth Street. Fourth Avenue was then Bowery Road, and the main entrance to the Garden was on that side, opposite the present Sixth Street. At Broadway the Garden narrowed down to a V shape. On this ground, for many years, John Sperry, a Swiss, cultivated fruits and flowers, and when he had grown old he sold his estate, in 1799, to John Jacob Astor. The latter leased it to a Frenchman named Delacroix, who had previously conducted the Vauxhall Garden on the Bayard Estate, close by the present Warren and Greenwich Streets. During the next eight years Delacroix transformed his newly-acquired possession into a pleasure garden, by erecting a small theatre and summer-house, and by setting out tables and seats under the trees on the grounds, and booths with benches around the inside close up to the high board fence that enclosed the Garden. He called the place Vauxhall, thereby causing some confusion to historians, who often confound this Garden with the earlier one of the same name. This last Vauxhall was situated a mile out of town on the Bowery Road. It was an attractive retreat, and the tableaux were so fine, the ballets so ingenious and the singing of such excellence, that the resort became immensely popular, and remained so continuously until the Garden was swept out of existence in 1855. Admission to the grounds was free, and to the theatre two shillings. In its last years it was a favorite place for the holding of large public meetings.

Cooper Union

Cooper Union. The Miriam and Ira D. Wallach Division of Art, Prints and Photographs: Photography Collection, NYPL Digital Collections, https://digitalcollections.nypl.org/items/510d47e1-ebce-a3d9-e040-e00a18064a99.

Cooper Union, at the upper end of the Bowery, was built in 1854 Peter Cooper, merchant and philanthropist, made the object of his life the establishment of an institution designed especially to give the working classes opportunity for self-education better than the existing institutions afforded. His store was on the site of the present building, which he founded. By a deed executed in 1859 the institution, with its incomes, he devoted to the instruction and improvement of the people of the United States forever. The institution has been taxed to its full capacity since its inception. From time to time it has been enriched by gifts from Mr. Cooper's heirs and friends. The statue of Peter Cooper, in the little park in front of the building, was unveiled May 28th, 1897. It is the work of Augustus St. Gaudens, once a pupil in the Institute.

On a part of the site of Cooper Union, at the east side of what was then the Bowery, and what is now Fourth Avenue, stood a house which was said to have been haunted. It was demolished to make way for Cooper Union. No permanent tenant, it is said, had occupied it for sixty years. It was a peaked-roofed brick structure, two stories high.

The house of Peter Cooper was on the site of the present Bible House, at Eighth Street and Third Avenue. He removed in 1820 to Twenty-eighth Street and Fourth Avenue, and his dwelling may still be seen there.

Peter Cooper's House, etching by by Charles Frederick William Mielatz. The Miriam and Ira D. Wallach Division of Art, Prints and Photographs: Print Collection, NYPL Digital Collections, https://digitalcollections.nypl.org/items/5e66b3e8-b078-d471-e040-e00a180654d7.

Astor Place

Astor Place is part of old Greenwich Lane, which led from the Bowery Lane past the pauper cemetery, where Washington Square is now, over the sand hills where University Place now is, and took the line of the present Greenwich Avenue. This was also called Monument Lane, because of a monument to the memory of General Wolfe erected on the spot where the road ended, at the junction of Eighth Avenue and Fifteenth Street.

Astor Place, as far as Fifth Avenue, was called Art Street when it was changed from a road to a street. The continuation of Astor Place to the east, now Stuyvesant Street, was originally Stuyvesant Road, and extended to the river at about Fifteenth Street. It was also called Art when it became a street. On the south side of this thoroughfare, just west of Fourth Avenue, Charlotte Temple lived in a small stone house.

At the head of Lafayette Place, fronting on Astor Place, is a building used at this time as a German Theatre. It was built for Dr. Schroeder, once the favorite preacher of the city, of whom it was said that if anyone desired to know where Schroeder preached, he had only to follow the crowds on Sunday. But he became dissatisfied and left Trinity for a church of his own. He very soon gave up this church, and for a time the building was occupied by St. Ann's Roman Catholic congregation. Afterward it became a theatre and failed to succeed.

The ground at the junction of Astor Place and Eighth Street was made a public square in 1836. In the midst of it may now be seen a statue of Samuel S. Cox.

Scene of Forrest-Macready Riots

Astor Place Opera House, at the junction of Eighth Street and Astor Place, where Clinton Hall stands now, was built in 1847. It was a handsome theatre for those days, and contained eighteen hundred seats. It was opened on November 22nd with "Ernani." On May 7th, 1849, at this house occurred the first of the Macready riots. The bitter jealousy existing between William Charles Macready, the English actor, and Edwin Forrest, which had assumed the proportions of an international quarrel, so far as the two actors and their friends were concerned, was the cause. The admirers of Forrest sought, on this night, to prevent the performance of "Macbeth," and a riot ensued in which no particular damage was done. On May 10th, in response to a petition signed by many prominent citizens, Macready again sought to play "Macbeth." An effort was made to keep all Forrest sympathizers from the house. Many, however, gained admission, and the performance was again frustrated. The ringleaders were arrested. A great crowd blocked Astor Place, and an assault upon the theatre was attempted. Macready escaped by a rear door. The Seventh Regiment and a troop of cavalry cleared Eighth Street and reached Astor Place. The mob resisted. The Riot Act was read. That producing no effect, and the assault upon the building and the soldiers defending it becoming more violent each moment, the mob was fired upon.

Astor Place Opera House Riot, May 10, 1849. The Miriam and Ira D. Wallach Division of Art, Prints and Photographs: Print Collection, NYPL Digital Collections.

Three volleys were fired. Thirty-four persons were killed and some hundred injured. Over one hundred soldiers and many policemen were also hurt.

On August 30th, 1852, the name of the house was changed to the New York Theatre, under the direction of Charles R. Thorne. In a month's time he gave up the venture and Frank Chanfrau took it up. He also abandoned it after a few weeks.

Clinton Hall

In 1854 the Opera House was reconstructed and occupied by the Mercantile Library. It was given the name of Clinton Hall, which had been the name of the library's first home in Beekman Street. This building in time gave way to the present Clinton Hall on the same site.

Lafayette Place

Lafayette Place was opened through the Vauxhall Garden in 1826.

The Astor Library, in Lafayette Place, was completed in 1853, and was opened in 1854. The site cost $25,000.

The Middle Dutch Reformed Church was built in Lafayette Place in 1839, at the northwest corner of Fourth Street after its removal from Nassau and Cedar Streets. A new church was built at Seventh Street and Second Avenue in 1844. In the Lafayette Place building was a bell which had been cast in Holland in 1731, and which had first been used when the church was in Nassau Street. It was the gift of Abraham de Peyster, and now hangs in the Reformed Church at Fifth Avenue and Forty-eighth Street.

Next to this church, for many years, lived Madam Canda, who kept the most fashionable school for ladies of a generation ago. Her beautiful daughter was dashed from a carriage, and killed on her eighteenth birthday—the age at which she was to make her debut into society. The entire city mourned her loss.

La Grange Terrace

La Grange Terrace. The Miriam and Ira D. Wallach Division of Art, Prints and Photographs: Print Collection, NYPL Digital Collections.

Soon after Lafayette Place was opened, La Grange Terrace was built. It was named after General Lafayette's home in France. The row is still prominent on the west side of the thoroughfare, and is known as Colonnade Row. A riot occurred at the time it was built, the masons of the city being aroused because the stone used in the structure was cut by the prisoners in Sing Sing prison.

John Jacob Astor lived on this street. He died March 29th, 1848, and was buried from the home of his son, William B. Astor, just south of the library building.

Sailors' Snug Harbor

A line drawn through Astor Place and continued to the Washington Arch in Washington Square, through Fifth Avenue to the neighborhood of Tenth Street, with Fourth Avenue as an eastern boundary, would roughly enclose what used to be the Eliot estate in the latter part of the eighteenth century. It was a farm of about twenty-one acres in 1790, when it was purchased for five thousand pounds from "Baron" Poelnitz, by Captain Robert Richard Randall, who had been a shipmaster and a merchant. Randall dying in 1801, bequeathed the farm for the founding of an asylum for superannuated sailors, together with the mansion house in which he had lived. The house stood, approximately, at the present northwest corner of Ninth Street and Broadway. It was the intention of Captain Randall that the Sailors' Snug Harbor should be built on the property, and the farming land used to raise all vegetables, fruit and grain necessary for the inmates. There were long years of litigation, however, for relatives contested the will. When the case was settled in 1831, the trustees had decided to lease the land, and to purchase the Staten Island property where the Asylum is now located. The estate at the time of Captain Randall's death) yielded an annual income of $4,000. At present the income is about $400,000 a year. It is conceded that the property would have increased more rapidly in value had it been sold outright, instead of becoming leasehold property in perpetuity.

Many efforts have been made to cut through Eleventh Street from Fourth Avenue to Broadway. The first was in 1830, when the street was open on the lines of the City Plan. Hendrick Brevoort, whose farm adjoined the Sailors' Snug Harbor property, had a homestead directly in the line of the proposed street, between Fourth Avenue and Broadway. He resisted the attempted encroachment on his home so successfully that the street was not opened through that block. He was again similarly successful in

1849 when an ordinance was passed for the removal of his house and the opening of the street.

Grace Church

Grace Church and Stewarts Store, c. 1920. The Miriam and Ira D. Wallach Division of Art, Prints and Photographs: Photography Collection, New York Public Library.

Grace Church, at Tenth Street and Broadway, was completed in 1846. Previous to that date it had been on the southwest corner of Broadway and Rector Street, opposite Trinity Church.

There is a reason for the sudden bend in Broadway at Tenth Street, close by Grace Church. The Bowery Lane, which is now Fourth Avenue, curved in passing through what is now Union Square until, at the line of the present Seventeenth Street it turned and took a direct course north and was from there-on called the Bloomingdale Road. This road to Bloomingdale was opened long before Broadway, and it was in order to let the latter connect as directly as possible with the straight road north that the direction of Broadway was changed about 1806 by the Tenth Street bend and a junction effected with the other road at the Seventeenth Street line.

At Thirteenth Street and Fourth Avenue there was constructed in 1834 a tank which was intended to furnish water for extinguishing fires. It had a capacity of 230,000 gallons, and was one hundred feet above tide water. Water was forced into it by a 12-horse power engine from a well and conducting galleries at the present Tenth Street and Sixth Avenue, on the site of the Jefferson Market Prison.

Wallack's Theatre

In 1861 James W. Wallack moved from Wallack's Lyceum at Broome Street, and occupied the new Wallack's, now the Star Theatre, at Thirteenth Street and Broadway. His last appearance was when he made a little speech at the close of the season of 1862. He died in 1864.

Union Square

Union Square. Irma and Paul Milstein Division of United States History, Local History and Genealogy, NYPL Digital Collections.

Union Square was provided for in the City Plan, under the name of Union Place. The Commissioners decided that the Place was necessary, as an opening for fresh air would be needed when the city should be built up. Furthermore, the union of so many roads intersecting at that point required space for convenience; and if the roads were continued without interruption the land would be divided into such small portions as to be valueless for building purposes.

The fountain in the square was operated for the first time in 1842, on the occasion of the great Croton Water celebration.

The bronze equestrian statue of Washington was erected in the square close by where the citizens had received the Commander of the Army when he entered the city on Evacuation Day, November 25, 1783. The statue is the work of Henry K. Brown. The dedication occurred on July 4, 1856, and was an imposing ceremony. Rev. George W. Bethune delivered an oration, and there was a military parade.

Academy of Music

The Academy of Music, at Fourteenth Street and Irving Place, was built in 1854 by a number of citizens who desired a permanent home for opera. On October 2nd of that year, Hackett took his company, headed by Grisi and Matio, there, the weather being too cold to continue the season at Castle Garden. The building was burned in 1866 and rebuilt in 1868.

In Third Avenue, between Sixteenth and Seventeenth Streets, is an old milestone which marked the third mile from Federal Hall on the Post Road.

The Friends' Meeting House, at East Sixteenth Street and Rutherford Place, has existed since 1860. In 1775 it was in Pearl Street, near Franklin Square. In 1824 it was taken down and rebuilt in 1826 in Rose Street, near Pearl.

St. George's Church

St. George's (Episcopal) Church, at Rutherford Place and Sixteenth Street, was built in 1845. The church was organized in 1752, and before occupying the present site was in Beekman Street.

Early in the century a stream of water ran from Stuyvesant's Pond, close by what is now Fourteenth Street and Second Avenue, to First Avenue and Nineteenth Street, having an outlet into the East River at about Sixteenth Street. In winter this furnished an excellent skating-ground.

Gramercy Park

Gramercy Park. Library of Congress Prints and Photographs Division, Washington, DC.

Gramercy Park, at Twentieth and Twenty-first Streets and Lexington Avenue, was originally part of the Gramercy Farm. In 1831 it was given by Samuel B. Ruggles to be used exclusively by the owners of lots fronting on it. It was laid out and improved in 1840. In the pavement, in front of the park gate on the west side, is a stone bearing this inscription:

GRAMERCY PARK
FOUNDED BY
SAMUEL B. RUGGLES
1831
COMMEMORATED BY THE TABLET
IMBEDDED IN
THE GRAMERCY FARM BY
JOHN RUGGLES STRONG.
1875.

Madison Square

There was no evidence during the last part of the eighteenth century that the town would ever creep up to and beyond the point where Twenty-third Street crosses Broadway. This point was the junction of the Post Road to Boston and the Bloomingdale Road. The latter was the fashionable out-of-town driveway, and it followed the course that Broadway and the Boulevard take now. The Post Road extended to the northeast. At this point, in 1794, a Potter's Field was established. There were many complaints at its being located there, where pauper funerals clashed with the vehicles of the well-to-do, and there was much rejoicing three years later, when the burying-ground was removed to the spot that is now Washington Square.

Arsenal in Madison Square

In 1797 was built, where the burying-ground had been, an arsenal which extended from Twenty-fourth Street and over the site of the Worth Monument. In the City Plan, completed in 1811, provision was made for a parade-ground to extend from Twenty-third to Thirty-fourth Streets, and Seventh to Third Avenue. The Commissioners decided that such a space was needed for military exercises, and where, in case of necessity, there could be assembled a force to defend the city. In 1814, the limits of the parade-ground were reduced to the space between Twenty-third and Thirty-first Streets, Sixth and Fourth Avenues, and given the name of Madison Square.

House of Refuge

The Arsenal in Madison Square was turned into a House of Refuge in 1824, and opened January 1, 1825. This was the result of the work of an association of citizens who formed a society to improve the condition of juvenile delinquents. The House of Refuge was burned in 1839, and another institution built at the foot of Twenty-third Street the same year. A portion of the old outer wall of this last structure is still to be seen on the north side of Twenty-third Street, between First Avenue and Avenue A.

In 1845, at the suggestion of Mayor James Harper, Madison Square was reduced to its present limits and laid out as a public park. Up to this time a stream of water had crossed the square, fed by springs in the district about Sixth Avenue, between Twenty-first and Twenty-seventh Streets. It spread out into a pond in Madison Square, and emptied into the East River at Seventeenth Street. It was suggested that a street be created over its bed from Madison Avenue to the river. This was not carried out, and the stream was simply buried.

Post Road

The road which branched out of the Bloomingdale Road at Twenty-third Street, sometimes called the Boston Post Road, sometimes the Post Road, sometimes the Boston Turnpike, ran across the present Madison Square, striking Fourth Avenue at Twenty-ninth Street; went through Kipsborough which hugged the river between Thirty-third and Thirty-seventh Streets, swept past Turtle Bay at Forty-seventh Street and the East River, crossed Second Avenue at Fifty-second Street, recrossed at Sixty-third Street, reached the Third Avenue line at Sixty-fifth Street, and at Seventy-seventh Street crossed a small stream over the Kissing Bridge. Then proceeded irregularly on this line to One Hundred and Thirtieth Street, where it struck the bridge over the Harlem River at Third Avenue. The road was closed in 1839.

The monument to Major-General William J. Worth, standing to the west of Madison Square, was dedicated November 25, 1857. General Worth was the main support of General Scott in the campaign of Mexico. His body was first interred in Greenwood Cemetery. On November 23rd the remains were taken to City Hall, where they lay in state for two days, then were taken, under military escort, and deposited beside the monument.

Fifth Avenue Hotel

Fifth Avenue Hotel. Rare Book Division, NYPL Digital Collections.

For twenty years, or more, prior to 1853, the site of the present Fifth Avenue Hotel, at Twenty-third Street and Broadway, was occupied by a frame cottage with a peaked roof, and covered veranda reached by a flight of wooden stairs. This was the inn of Corporal Thompson, and a favorite stopping-place on the Bloomingdale Road. An enclosed lot, extending as far as the present Twenty-fourth Street, was used at certain times of the year for cattle exhibitions. In 1853 the cottage made way for Franconi's Hippodrome, a brick structure, two stories high, enclosing an open space two hundred and twenty-five feet in diameter. The performances given here were considered of great merit and received with much favor. In 1856 the Hippodrome was removed, and in 1858 the present Fifth Avenue Hotel was opened.

The Madison Square Presbyterian Church, at Madison Avenue and Twenty-fourth Street, was commenced in 1853, the earlier church of the congregation having been in Broome Street. It was opened December, 1854, with Rev. Dr. William Adams as pastor.

College of City of New York

At the southeast corner of Twenty-third Street and Lexington Avenue, the College of the City of New York has stood since 1848, the opening exercises having taken place in 1849. In 1847 the Legislature passed an Act authorizing the establishment of a free academy for the benefit of pupils who had been educated in the public schools of this city. The name Free Academy was given to the institution, and under that name it was incorporated. It had the power to confer degrees and diplomas. In 1866 the name was changed to its present title, and all the privileges and powers of a college were conferred upon it. In 1882 the college was thrown open to all young men, whether educated in the public schools of this city or not. In 1898 ground was set aside in the northern part of the city, overlooking the Hudson River, for the erection of modern buildings suitable to meet the growth of the college.

Old House of Refuge Wall

The House of Refuge in Madison Square was, after the fire in 1839, rebuilt on the block bounded by Twenty-third and Twenty-fourth Streets, First Avenue and the East River. It was surrounded by a high wall, a section of which is still standing on the north side of Twenty-third Street, between First Avenue and Avenue A. The river at that time extended west to beyond the Avenue A line. The old gateway is there yet, and is used now as the entrance to a coal-yard. Some of the barred windows of the wall can still be seen. In 1854 the inmates were removed to Randall's Island, and were placed in charge of the State.

GATE of
Old House of Refuge

Bellevue Hospital

Bellevue Hospital has occupied its present site, at the foot of East Twenty-sixth Street, since about 1810. The hospital really had its beginning in 1736, in the buildings of the Public Workhouse and House of Correction in City Hall Park. There were six beds there, in charge of the medical officer, Dr. John Van Beuren. About the beginning of the nineteenth century, yellow fever patients were sent to a building known as Belle Vue, on the Belle Vue Farm, close by the present hospital buildings. In about 1810 it was decided to establish a new almshouse, penitentiary and hospital on the Belle Vue Farm. Work on this was completed in 1816. The almshouse building was three stories high, surmounted by a cupola, and having a north and south wing each one hundred feet long. This original structure stands to-day, and is part of the present hospital building, other branches having been added to it from time to time. The water line, at that time, was within half a block of where First Avenue is now.

In 1848 the Almshouse section of the institution was transferred to Blackwell's Island. The ambulance service was started in 1869, and was the first service of its kind in the world.

Bull's Head Village

Bull's Head Village was located in the district now included within Twenty-third and Twenty-seventh Streets, Fourth and Second Avenues. It became a centre of importance in 1826, when the old Bull's Head Tavern was moved from its early home on the Bowery, near Bayard Street, to the point which is now marked by Twenty-sixth Street and Third Avenue. It continued to be the headquarters of drovers and stockmen. As at that time there was no bank north of the City Hall Park, the Bull's Head Tavern served as inn, bank and general business emporium for the locality. For more than twenty years this district was the great cattle market of the city. As business increased, stores and business houses were erected, until, toward the year 1850, the cattle mart, which was the source of all business, was crowded out. It was moved up-town to the neighborhood of Forty-second Street; later to Ninety-fourth Street, and in the early 80's to the Jersey shore. The most celebrated person connected with the management of the Bull's Head Tavern was Daniel Drew. He afterwards operated in Wall Street, became a director of the New York and Erie Railroad upon its completion in 1851, and accumulated a fortune by speculation.

Peter Cooper's House

At Twenty-eighth Street and Fourth Avenue, on the southeast corner, the house numbered 399-401, stands the old "Cooper Mansion," in which Peter Cooper lived. It was formerly on the site where the Bible House is now, at the corner of Eighth Street and Fourth Avenue. Peter Cooper himself super-intended the removal of the house in 1820, and directed its establishment on the new site so that it should be reconstructed in a manner that should absolutely preserve its original form. Now it presents an insignificant appearance crowded about by modern structures, and it is occupied by a restaurant.

This corner of Twenty-eighth Street and Fourth Avenue was directly on the line of the Boston Post Road. Just at that point the Middle Road ran from it, and extended in a direct line to Fifth Avenue and Forty-second Street.

Little Church Around the Corner

The Little Church Around the Corner, allow rambling structure, seemingly all angles and corners, is on the north side of Twenty-ninth Street, midway of the block between Fifth and Madison Avenues. It is the Episcopal

Church of The Transfiguration. Its picturesque title was bestowed upon it in 1871, when Joseph Holland, an English actor, the father of E. M. and Joseph Holland, the players known to the present generation, died. Joseph Jefferson, when arranging for the funeral, went to a church which stood then at Madison Avenue and Twenty-eighth Street, to arrange for the services. The minister said that his congregation would object to an actor being buried from their church, adding: "But there is a little church around the corner where they have such funerals." Mr. Jefferson, astonished that such petty and unjust distinctions should be persisted in even in the face of death, exclaimed: "All honor to that Little Church Around the Corner !" From that time until the present day, "The Little Church Around the Corner" has been the religious refuge of theatrical folk. For twenty-six years of that time, and until his death, the Rev. Dr. George H. Houghton, who conducted the services over the remains of actor Holland, was the firm friend of the people of the stage in times of trouble, of sickness and of death.

Lich Gate

The lich gate at the entrance of the church is unique in this country, and is considered the most elaborate now in existence anywhere. It was erected in 1895, at a cost of $4,000.

The congregation worshipped first in a house at No. 48 East Twenty-fourth Street, in 1850. The present building was opened in 1856. Lester Wallack was buried from this church, as were Dion Boucicault, Edwin Booth, and a host of others. In the church is a memorial window to the memory of Edwin Booth, which was unveiled in 1898. It represents a mediaeval histrionic student, his gaze fixed on a mask in his hand. Below the figure is the favorite quotation of Booth, from "Henry II": "As one, in suffering all, that suffers nothing; a man that fortune's buffets and rewards has taken with equal thanks." And the further inscription: "To the glory of God and in loving memory of Edwin Booth this window has been placed here by 'The Players.'"

At Lexington Avenue and Thirtieth Street is the First Moravian Church, which has occupied the building since 1869. This congregation was established in 1749. In 1751 their first church was built at No. 108 Fair (now Fulton) Street. In 1829 a second house was erected on the same site. In 1849 a new building was erected at the southwest corner of Houston and Mott Streets. This property was sold in 1865, and the congregation then worshipped in the Medical College Hall, at the northwest corner of

Twenty-third Street and Fourth Avenue, until the purchase of the present building from the Episcopalians. It was erected by the Baptists in 1825.

Brick Presbyterian Church

At Fifth Avenue and Thirty-seventh Street is the Brick Presbyterian Church, which stood at the junction of Park Row and Nassau Street until 1858, when the present structure was erected. The locality was a very different one then, and the square quaintness of the church looks out of place amid its present modern surroundings. There is an air of solitude about it, as though it mourned faithfully for the green fields that shed peace and quietness about its walls when it was first built there.

It is related of William C. H. Waddell, who, in 1845, built a residence on the same site, that when he went to look at the plot, with a view to purchase, his wife waited for him near by, under the shade of an apple tree. The ground there was high above the city grade.

Bryant Park

Bryant Park; Croton Reservoir; Harmonie Club; West Presbyterian Church. Irma and Paul Milstein Division of United States History, Local History and Genealogy, New York Public Library.

The ground between Fifth and Sixth Avenues, Fortieth and Forty-second Streets, now occupied by Bryant Park and the old reservoir, was purchased by the city in 1822, and in 1823 a Potter's Field was established there, the one in Washington Square having been abandoned in its favor. The reservoir, of Egyptian architecture, was finished in 1842. Its cost was about $500,000. On July 5th water was introduced into it through the new Croton aqueduct, with appropriate ceremonies. The water is brought from the Croton lakes, forty-five miles above the city, through conduits of solid masonry. The first conduit, which was begun in 1835, is carried across the Harlem River through the High Bridge, which was erected especially to accommodate it. At the time the reservoir was put in use the locality was at the northern limits of the city. On Sundays and holidays people went on journeys to the reservoir, and from the promenades at the top of the structure had a good view from river to river, and of the city to the south. The reservoir has not been in use for many years.

The park was called Reservoir Square until 1884, when the name was changed to Bryant Park.

A World's Fair

On July 4, 1853, a World's Fair, in imitation of the Crystal Palace, near London, was opened in Reservoir Square, when President Pierce made an address. The fair was intended to set forth the products of the world, but it attracted but little attention outside the city. It was opened as a permanent exposition on May 14, 1854, but proved a failure. One of the attractions was a tower 280 feet high, which stood just north of the present line of Forty-second Street and Fifth Avenue. In August, 1856, it was burned, and as a great pillar of flame it attracted more attention than ever before. The exposition buildings and their contents were in the hands of a receiver when they were destroyed by fire October 5, 1858.

Bryant Park has been selected as the site for the future home of the consolidated Tilden, Astor and Lenox Libraries.

Murray Hill

Murray Hill derives its name from the possessions of Robert Murray, whose house, Inclenberg, stood at the corner of what is now Thirty-sixth

Street and Park Avenue, on a farm which lay between the present Thirty-third and Thirty-seventh Streets, Bloomingdale Road (now Broadway) and the Boston Post Road (the present Third Avenue). The house was destroyed by fire in 1834. On September 15, 1776, after the defeat on Long Island, the Americans were marching northward from the lower end of the island, when the British, marching toward the west, reached the Murray House. There the officers were well entertained by the Murrays, who, at the same time, managed to get word to the American army: the latter hurried on and joined Washington at about Forty-third Street and Broadway, before the English suspected that they were anywhere within reach.

The Murray Farm extended down to Kip's Bay at Thirty-sixth Street. The Kip mansion was the oldest house on the Island of Manhattan when it was torn down in 1851. Where it stood, at the crossing of Thirty-fifth Street and Second Avenue, there is now not a trace. Jacob Kip built the house in 1655, of brick which he imported from Holland. The locality between the Murray Hill Farm and the river, that is, east of what is now Third Avenue between Thirty-third and Thirty-seventh Streets, was called Kipsborough in Revolutionary times.

Turtle Bay

The British forces landed, on the day of the stop at the Murray House, in Turtle Bay, that portion of the East River between Forty-sixth and Forty-seventh Streets. It was a safe harbor and a convenient one. Overlooking the bay, on a great bluff at the present Forty-first Street, was the summer home of Francis Bayard Winthrop. He owned the Turtle Bay Farm. The bluff is there yet, and subsequent cutting through of the streets has left it in appearance like a small mountain peak. Winthrop's house is gone, and in its place is Corcoran's Roost, far up on the height, whose grim wall of stone on the Fortieth Street side at First Avenue became in modern times the trysting place for members of the "Rag Gang."

The Elgin Garden

Elgin Garden. The Miriam and Ira D. Wallach Division of Art, Prints and Photographs: Print Collection, New York Public Library.

Forty-seventh and Forty-ninth Streets, between Fifth and Sixth Avenues, enclose the tract formerly known as the Elgin Garden. This was a botanical garden founded by David Hosack, M.D., in 1801, when he was Professor of Botany in Columbia College. In 1814 the land was purchased by the State from Dr. Hosack and given to Columbia College, in consideration of lands which had been owned by the College but ceded to New Hampshire after the settlement of the boundary dispute. The ground is still owned by Columbia University.

The block east of Madison Avenue, between Forty-ninth and Fiftieth Streets, was occupied in 1857 by Columbia College, when the latter moved from its down-town site at Church and Murray Streets. The College occupied the building which had been erected in 1817 by the founders of the Institute for the Instruction of the Deaf and Dumb—the first asylum for mutes in the United States. The original intention had been to erect the college buildings on a portion of the Elgin Garden property, but the expense involved was found to be too great. The asylum property, consisting of twenty lots and the buildings, was purchased in 1856. Subsequently the remainder of the block was also bought up.

St. Patrick's Cathedral

At Fiftieth Street and Fifth Avenue is St. Patrick's Cathedral, the cornerstone of which was laid in 1858. The entire block on which it stands was, the preceding year, given to the Roman Catholics for a nominal sum—one dollar—by the city.

The Roman Catholic Orphan Asylum in the adjoining block, on Fifth Avenue, between Fifty-first and Fifty-second Streets, was organized in 1825, but not incorporated until 1852, when the present buildings were erected.

Four Mile Stone

There is still standing, in Third Avenue, just above Fifty-seventh Street, a milestone. It was once on the Post Road, four miles from Federal Hall in Wall Street.

Mile-stone
3rd Ave. near 47th St.

Close by Fiftieth Street and Third Avenue, a Potter's Field was established about 1835. Near it was a spring of exceptionally pure water. This water was carried away in carts and supplied to the city. Even after the introduction of Croton water the water from this spring commanded a price of two cents a pail from many who were strongly prejudiced against water that had been supplied through pipes.

Beekman House

Memories of Nathan Hale, the Martyr Spy of the Revolution, hover about the neighborhood of Fifty-first Street and First Avenue. The Beekman House stood just west of the Avenue, between Fifty-first and Fifty-second Streets, on the site where Grammar School No. 135 is now. It was in a room of this house that Major Andre slept, and in the morning passed out to dishonor; and it was in a greenhouse on these grounds that Nathan Hale passed the last of his nights upon earth. The house was built in 1763 by a descendant of the William Boekman who came from Holland in 1647 with Peter Stuyvesant. During the Revolution it was the headquarters of General Charles Clinton and Sir William Howe. It stood until 1874, by which time it had degenerated into a crumbling tenement, and was demolished when it threatened to fall of natural decay.

An Old Shot Tower

A very few steps from the East River, at Fifty-third Street, stands an old brick shot tower; a lonely and neglected sentinel now, but still proudly looking skyward and bearing witness to its former usefulness. It was built in 1821 by a Mr. Youle. On October 9th it was nearing completion when it collapsed. It was at once rebuilt, and, as has been said, still stands. In 1827, Mr. Youle advertised the sale of the lots near the tower, and designated the location as being "close by the Old Post Road near the four mile stone."

The De Voor Farm

Within half a dozen steps of the old tower, in the same lumber yard, is a house said to be the oldest in the city. It is of Dutch architecture, with sloping roof and a wide porch. The cutting through and grading of Fifty-third Street have forced it higher above the ground than its builders intended it to be. The outer walls, in part, have been hoarded over, and some "modern improvements" have made it somewhat unsightly; but inside, no vandal's art has been sufficient to hide its solid oak beams and its stone foundations that have withstood the shocks of time successfully. It was a farm-house, and its site was the Spring Valley Farm of the Revolution. It is thought to have been built by some member of the De Voor family, who, after 1677, had a grant of sixty acres of land along the river, and gave their name to a millstream long since forgotten, save for allusion in the pages of history.

A block away in Fifty-fourth Street, between First Avenue and the river, is another Dutch house, though doubtless of much later origin. It stands back from the street and has become part of a brewery, being literally surrounded by buildings.

Central Park

The first suggestion of a Central Park was made in the fall of 1850, when Andrew J. Downing, writing to the *Horticulturist*, advocated the establishment of a large park because of the lack of recreation-grounds in the city. On April 5, 1851, Mayor Ambrose C. Kingsland, in a special message to the Common Council, suggested the necessity for the new park, pointing out the limited extent and inadequacy of the existing ones. The Common Council, approving of the idea, asked the Legislature for authority to secure the necessary land. The ground suggested for the new park was the property known as "Jones' Woods," which lay between Sixty-sixth and Seventy-fifth Streets, Third Avenue and the East River. At an extra session of the Legislature in July, 1851, an Act known as the "Jones' Woods Park Bill" was passed, under which the city was given the right to acquire the land. The passage of this Act opened a discussion as to whether there was no other location better adapted for a public park than Jones' Woods. In August a committee was appointed by the Board of Aldermen to examine the proposed plot and others. This committee reported in favor of what they considered a more central site, namely, the ground lying between Fifty-ninth and One Hundred and Sixth Streets, Fifth and Eighth Avenues. On July 23, 1853, the Legislature passed an Act giving authority for the acquirement of the land, afterward occupied by Central Park, to Commissioners appointed by the Supreme Court. The previous Jones' Woods Act was repealed. These Commissioners awarded for damages $5,169, 369.69, and for benefits $1,657,590.00, which report was confirmed by the court in February, 1856.

In May, 1856, the Common Council appointed a commission which took charge of the work of construction. On this commission were William C. Bryant, Washington Irving and George Bancroft. In 1857, however, a new Board was appointed by the Legislature, because of the inactivity of the first one. Under the new Board, in April of the year in which they were appointed, the designs of Calvert Vaux and Frederick L. Olmsted were accepted and actual work was begun.

The plans for the improvement of the park, which have been consistently adhered to, were based upon the natural configuration of the land. As nearly as possible the hills, valleys and streams were preserved undisturbed. Trees, shrubs and vines were arranged with a view to an harmonious blending of size, shape and color—all that would attract the eye and make the park as beautiful in every detail as in its entirety.

The year 1857 was one of much distress to the poor, and work on the park being well under way, the Common Council created employment for many laborers by putting them to work grading the new park.

The original limits were extended from One Hundred and Sixth to One Hundred and Tenth Street in 1859.

As it exists to-day, Central Park contains eight hundred and sixty-two acres, of which one hundred and eighty-five and one-quarter are water. It is two and a half miles long and half a mile wide. Five hundred thousand trees have been set out since the acquisition of the land. There are nine miles of carriageway, five and a half miles of bridle-path, twenty-eight and one half miles of walk, thirty buildings, forty-eight bridges, tunnels and archways, and out-of-door seats for ten thousand persons. It is assessed at $87,000,000 and worth twice that amount. More than $14,000,-000 have been spent on improvements.

AFTERWORD

Ken Bloom

New York is an ever-changing city. Every day old buildings are demolished and new ones take their place. That's what gives the city its drive, constantly moving forward, ever reinventing itself. But thanks to the vagaries of commerce and community with a boost from preservation groups, some landmarks survive the onslaught of time.

Published in 1899, *Nooks and Corners of Old New York* heralds the historic buildings of New York's earliest decades. Its author, Charles Hemstreet, wrote several popular histories of New York City and its environs, having trained as a newspaper reporter. *Nooks and Corners* was probably his most popular book and one that has continued to draw readers for its concise retelling of New York's early history. Hemstreet's descriptions of these buildings and their purpose lets us see New York in its infancy, before becoming the most important port in the country—and the growth in wealth and culture that ensued.

The original volume was enhanced by drawings by well-known illustrator E.C. (Ernest Clifford) Peixotto. Peixotto was a regular contributor to the popular *Scribner's Magazine*, and also an author of travel literature. He was well-known for his evocative renditions of historic buildings, often capturing the neighboring street life to give a sense of how these buildings related to their environment.

Hemstreet was a true advocate for historic preservation, and it was with an eye toward preserving New York's history that he wrote the original text. Even before this book was published, New York was losing its historic landmarks. In 1856, *Harper's Magazine* bemoaned the destruction of the past: "Why should (New York) be loved as a city? It is never the same city for a dozen years together. A man born in New York forty years ago finds nothing, absolutely nothing, of the New York he knew." The loss of early buildings lead some to advocate for preserving the city's history, particularly as it grew in wealth and stature through the late 19th century.

Andrew Haswell Green was a lawyer who became active in New York City planning, spearheading the movement to establish Central Park. In 1894, he rallied a group of business leaders to save City Hall from being torn down. A year later, he launched New York's first formal conservation group, later named, the American Scenic and Historic Preservation Society (ASHPS). Through the years, members of the society were behind the establishment of the Municipal Art Society, the Fine Arts Federation, and the National Arts Club. J.P. Morgan gave the organization an endowment. Two years later, in 1897, the Colonial Dames of the State of New York took a lease on the 1748 Van Cortlandt mansion and set upon restoring it. In 1899, the Van Cortlandt family gave the mansion to the City of New York. Another woman's organization, the Daughters of the American Revolution, the "Dames" rivals, insisted the city buy the Morris–Jumel Mansion, where George Washington directed the Battle of Harlem Heights. In 1912, the ASHPS noted that, "in the midst of the many changes in our fluid city we need some permanent landmarks to suggest stability." And that started a new wave of interest in historic buildings.

These organizations and others had an impact, but still historic New York was disappearing. In 1908, Trinity Church decided to redevelop the land on which their St. John's Chapel stood. A petition, signed by such luminaries as President Roosevelt, Elihu Root, J.P. Morgan, and others, argued for the preservation of the chapel. But Trinity rejected the idea, and the chapel was demolished. The church's reputation was further darkened by its ownership of blocks and blocks of New York tenements, housing the poor in appalling conditions. It owned a dozen tenements on Clarkson Street, 66 tenement buildings on Varick Street, 51 tenements on West Houston, 65 on upper Greenwich Street, 26 on Charlton Street, 47 on Canal Street, 22 on Barrow Street, and 138 properties on Vandam Street. The value of this land was estimated to be between 39 million and 100 million.

Despite all of the changes in New York City's streetscape over the past decades, surprisingly several of the landmarks covered in the book are still around today. Some have hardly changed while others have weathered the years by adaptation and reuse.

No. 7 State Street is the location of the James Watson house. The building was erected in 1793 for Watson who was the first Speaker of the New York State Assembly and a member of the New York and United States Senates. He built his house close to the East River and access to the ocean, which made sense since he made his money through his import/export business. In those days, before landfills, Watson's house was close enough to the water to provide him a view of his ships.

In 1806, Watson sold his house to Moses Rogers. Rogers' in-law was shipping magnate Archibald Gracie (after whom Gracie Mansion is named). When the hoi polloi moved uptown, State Street was no longer a preferred address and first the Ithaca steamship line and then the US government took over while the Civil War was still raging. Afterward, the Harbor's Pilot Commissioners was lodged in the house. From 1885, it housed a home for emigrant Irish girls founded by the Catholic church.

Bowling Green Park still exists though it has changed over the years since its creation in 1733. The area was first occupied by the Lenape Native American tribe. It's said that in 1626, Dutch Governor Peter Minuit purchased Manhattan from the tribe for $24 of merchandise. The city of New Amsterdam held a cattle market in the area between 1638 and 1647. The site also held Fort Amsterdam and in 1677, the city's first well was dug there. Part of the park was leased to neighbors who paid the extravagant sum of one peppercorn for the right to create a park. The park was dedicated to, "the beauty and ornament of said streets as well as the recreation and delight of the inhabitants."

The British government claimed New Amsterdam and erected a gilded statue of King George astride a horse and wearing a Roman uniform. It weighed two tons. The statue proved to be a hindrance when that same year of 1770, mass protests against the British were held around the statue. Three years later the British enacted laws forbidding graffiti and any harm to the statue and erected a cast iron fence at the edges of the park.

In 1776, Washington's troops heard the Declaration of Independence read to them by what is now City Hall. The crowd ran to the park and destroyed the statue of the King. The iron was melted down to make 42,000 bullets that would be used against the British. Relics of the statue can be found in New York museums, while its head was shipped to England. On November 25, 1783, the British Flag was ripped from its flagpole and an American flag was hoisted in its place.

Over the next decades the park deteriorated until, in 1972, restoration began. The park and the original fence were put on the list of the

National Register of Historic Place. Practically the only relic of the past that has made it to today is the original iron fence that was built by the British. Today's visitors to the park are confronted by the bronze Charging Bull statue sculpted by Arturo Di Modica. It was erected in 1989 as a symbol of the power of the New York Stock Exchange and Wall Street.

Governor's Island sits at the meeting of New York's two great rivers, the Hudson River and the East River. In 1698, the island was set aside "for the benefit and accommodation of His Majesty's governors." In succeeding years the island was put to use as a sheep farm, quarantine station, racetrack, and game preserve. Now the Coast Guard is in command and visitors are only allowed on two weekends per year. The island is reached by ferry boat, there being no bridge over the East River.

Fraunces's Tavern is New York's oldest building and is now a National Landmark. Samuel Fraunces was born Samuel Francis but after the British left New York with the help of the French, he took the French influenced name, Fraunces. He was a hero of the Revolutionary War, secretly helping prisoners of war; for his actions, Congress awarded him $2,000 "in consideration for singular services." General Washington appointed Fraunces as the Steward to the President. When Washington decided to retire to Mount Vernon, the French Ambassador threw a party in the building for the commander. One hundred and twenty guests drank 135 bottles of Madeira, 36 bottles of port, 60 bottles of English beer, and 30 bowls of punch.

Like many early buildings, the tavern was beset by a series of fires beginning in 1832. In 1845, the Buermeyer family leased the building and installed a hotel named the Broad Street House. Another fire claimed the building in 1852 and the reconstruction added two floors to the original three.

In 1900, plans were made to tear down the tavern in favor of a parking lot. However, the state used eminent domain to save the building. Because the rules of municipal ordinances didn't recognize buildings in the statutes, the tavern was deemed a park. In 1904, the Sons of the Revolution in the State of New York purchased the building and restored its structure. Three years later the building's reconstruction was complete. Part of the change was the elimination of the two previously constructed upper stories and a pitched roof, which came under some criticism. In 1965, the building was declared a Landmark. Today, it's a thriving bar catering to the Wall Street crowd. And there's a small museum on the history of the building.

Statue of Nathan Hale, City Hall Park, which is nine feet tall, was created in Paris and sent to the New York studio of artist August St. Gaudens where it went on display while a pedestal six feet tall was fashioned by Stanford White, the famed architect. On Evacuation Day, November 25, 1893, the Sons of the Revolution erected a bronze statue of the patriot at the corner of Broadway and Chambers Street. The statue, created by artist Frederick William MacMonnies, features Hale with his arms and legs bound by British loyalists. Later the statue was moved to its present position in front of the steps of City Hall, close by the spot where Hale was hanged.

Hale's arms and legs are bound as he awaits the hangman's noose. He is wearing a coat and waistcoat and a frilled shirt with the top buttons open ready for the ropes. Hale's last words have entered the history books, "I only regret that I have but one life to give for my country."

No. 11 Reade Street and Aaron Burr's Office were built on the site of the African Burial Ground. In 1795, a year after the cemetery was closed, the land was subdivided for houses. Burr had fled New York for England in 1804 after killing Alexander Hamilton in a duel. Eight years later he returned and set up residence on Reade Street. The citizens of New York had not forgotten the duel and business was terrible. Burr was quickly going bankrupt when Eliza Jumel, recently widowed from her husband, Samuel Jumel, made his acquaintance. They were quickly married, each having their own reasons for the nuptials. But, as *The New York Times* reported, "He abused her confidence, lost a portion of her fortune, and she summarily dismissed him within a year."

Over the years with many other tenants occupying it, the house deteriorated. In 1898, the house and its neighbors were demolished to make way for the new Hall of Records. *The Sun* newspaper reported, "tradition . . . even points out the spike holes in the wall by the door where (Burr's) shingle swung in sight of his legislative triumph."

Today's Manhattan Detention Complex sits in what was the historic neighborhood of Five Points. The Bridewell Prison first occupied the land in 1735. It was demolished in 1838 to make way for The Halls of Justice and House of Detention. That building was dubbed "**The Tombs**" because of its Egyptian inspired façade. The prison was plagued by corruption and horrible conditions. Eventually, it was replaced by a succession of prisons, each dubbed "The Tombs." The Halls of Justice was replaced by the City Prison from 1902 to 1941. From 1941 to 1974 stood the Manhattan House of Detention and from 1983 until the present sits the Manhattan Detention Complex (renamed the Bernard B. Kerik Complex in 2001).

Park Street and The Church of the Transfiguration still stand at Church and Park Street. Today the church is known as "the little church around the corner." Just before Christmas of 1870, Broadway star, Joseph Jefferson, was arranging for a funeral and burial plot for an actor friend of his, George Holland. Upon learning that the deceased was an actor, the rector refused to hold a funeral for the man at his church. The rector said, "I believe there is a little church around the corner where it might be done." And from then on it was known as "The Little Church Around the Corner" and was forever associated with actors. Even James Joyce referred to the "tin choorch round the coroner" and "ye litel church rond ye corner" in his classic novel, *Finnegans Wake*.

Erected in the era of gas lighting, the **Bowery Theatre** burned down four times in seventeen years. Even though the name changed over the years (Thalia Theatre, Fays' Bowery Theatre, etc.), people still called it the Bowery. The 1929 fire was its last.

Macomb's Mansion was built by Alexander Macomb from 1786 to 1788. Macomb was a merchant who also made money in real estate. Two years after its construction, he leased the house to the French Minister Plenipotentiary, the Comte de Moustier, who remained there until George Washington moved the capitol to Pennsylvania in 1790. In 1821, the house became a hotel, Mansion's House Hotel. Sadly, the house was torn down in 1940.

Tin Pot Alley—not to be confused with "Tin Pan Alley"—was one of the shortest streets in Manhattan, and only eighteen feet wide, when it was built. During the forty year long Dutch occupation of Manhattan, beginning in 1624, the street was called "Tuyn Paat," meaning "Garden Alley." When the British arrived they referred to the narrow lane as Tin Pot Alley. In 1795, the City of New York took over control and renamed it Edgar Street Greenstreet, after William Edgar, a successful shipper. It's now considered the shortest street in Manhattan.

St. Paul's Chapel is now known mainly for its proximity to the World Trade Center. When the complex was destroyed on September 11 2001, it became an important part of the City's culture. In the three-quarters of a year following the tragedy, the chapel provided twenty-four hour a day assistance to workers and firefighters, including food, beds, medical care from various professionals as well as support from religious figures offering counsel and prayers. Today the Chapel has become a favorite tourist destination with a video presentation and exhibits dealing with the tragedy.

Today, **Canal Street** starts at the entrance/exit of the Holland Tunnel and ends at the Manhattan Bridge to Brooklyn. Along the way it divides Little Italy and Soho on the north side to Chinatown and Tribeca on the south. The street is also known for its many peddlers offering knock-off watches, jewelry, and clothing.

La Grange Terrace is a stunning building now known as Colonnade Row. Currently four of the original nine row houses remain. The rest were torn down in 1902 to make room for a Wanamaker's department store. In 1965, the remaining part of the building was added to the National Register of Historic Places.

The second **Academy of Music** was erected after the original building burned down in 1866. A new structure was erected but by then the Metropolitan Opera House had opened in 1883 and the Academy couldn't compete. It was three years later that the Academy switched to vaudeville. In 1926, Con Edison built a new building on the site.

INDEX

www.ingramcontent.com/pod-product-compliance
Lightning Source LLC
LaVergne TN
LVHW041111090826
844660LV00057B/205

* 9 7 8 1 4 3 8 4 9 5 0 0 2 *